MAKEUP HALLOWEEN

TABLE OF CONTENTS

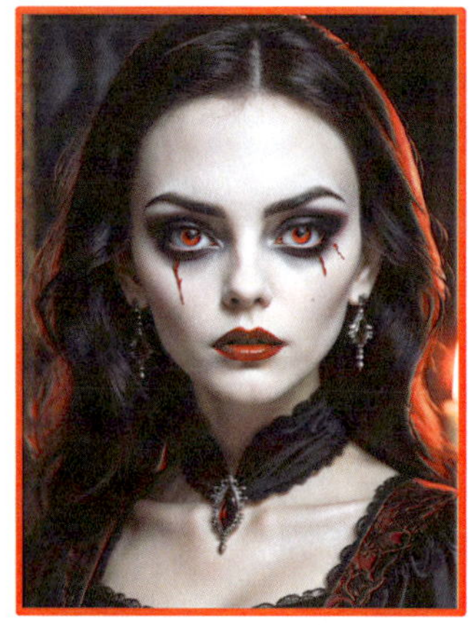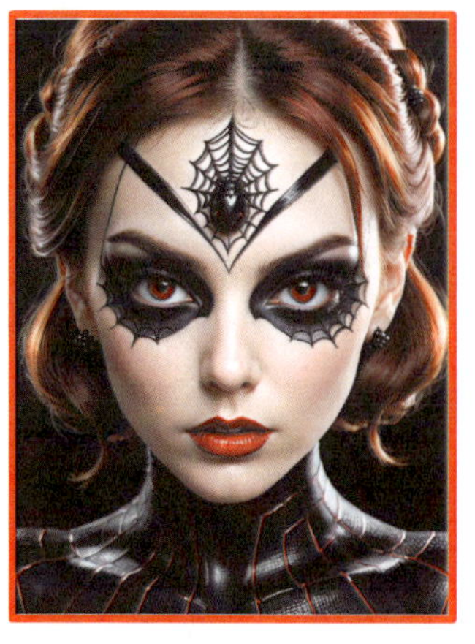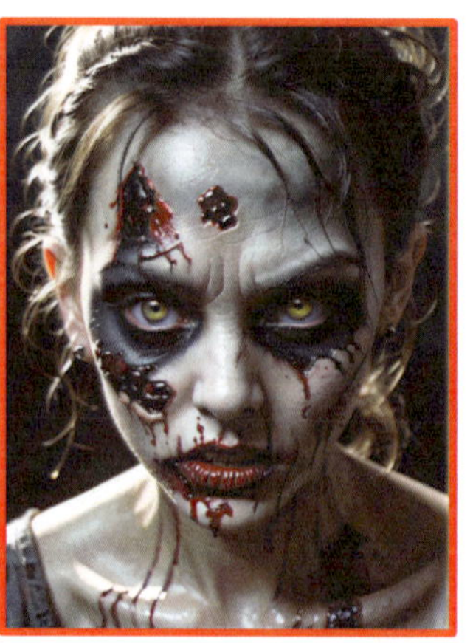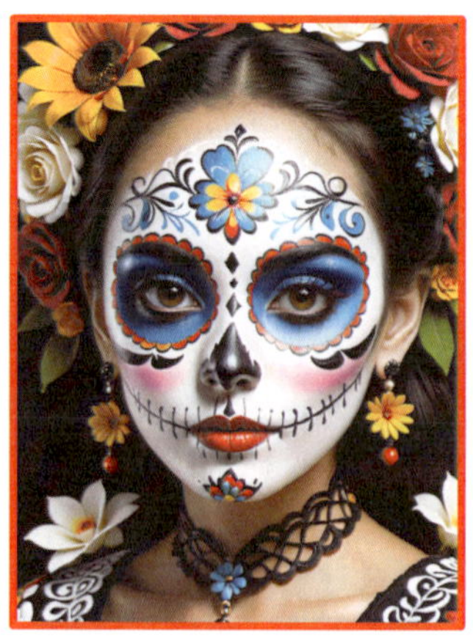
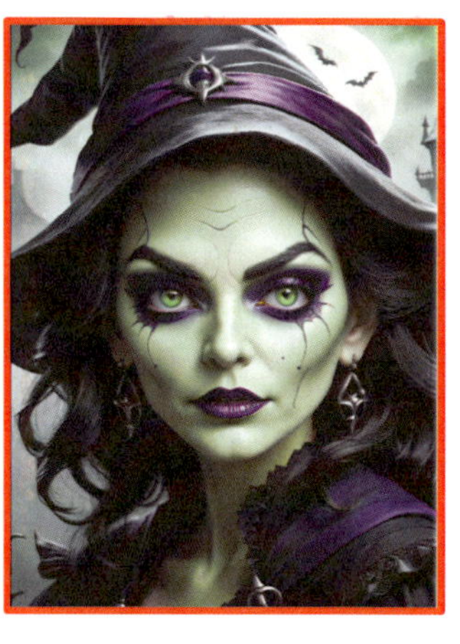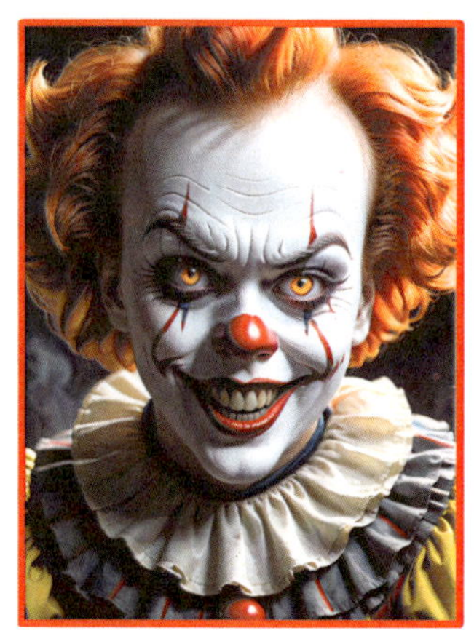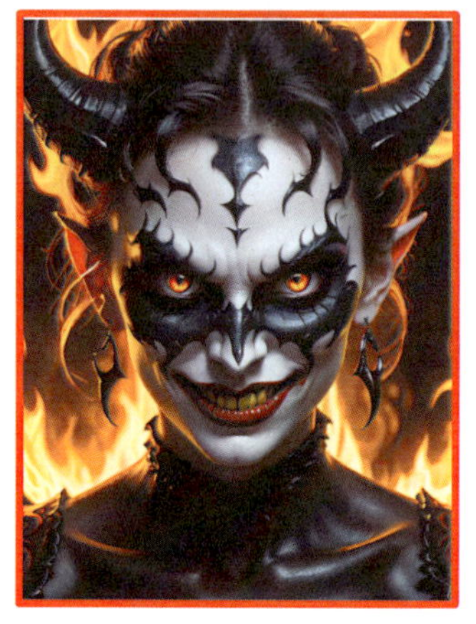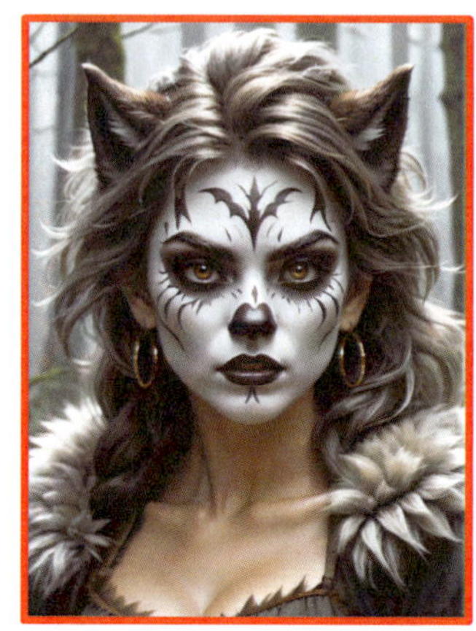
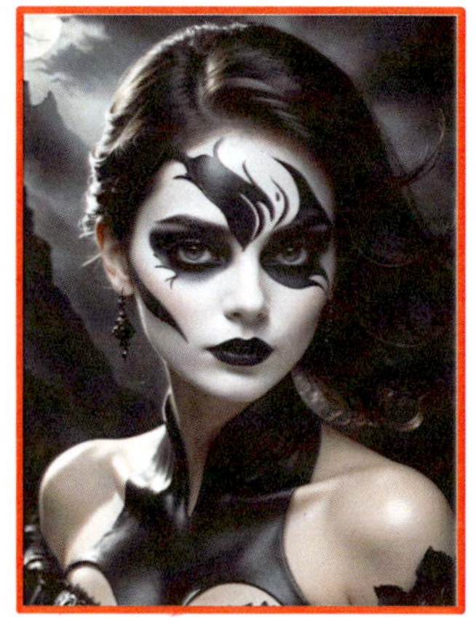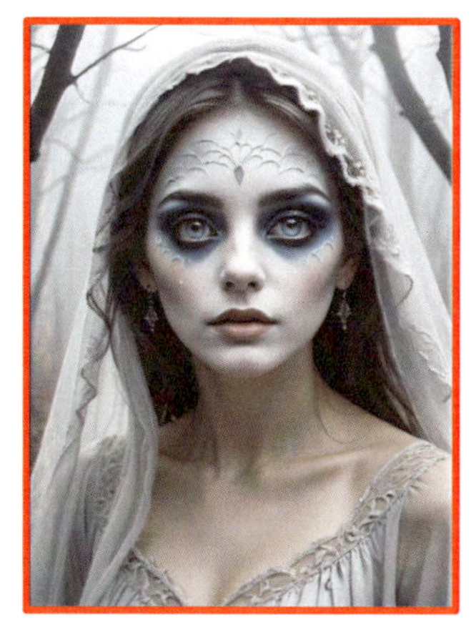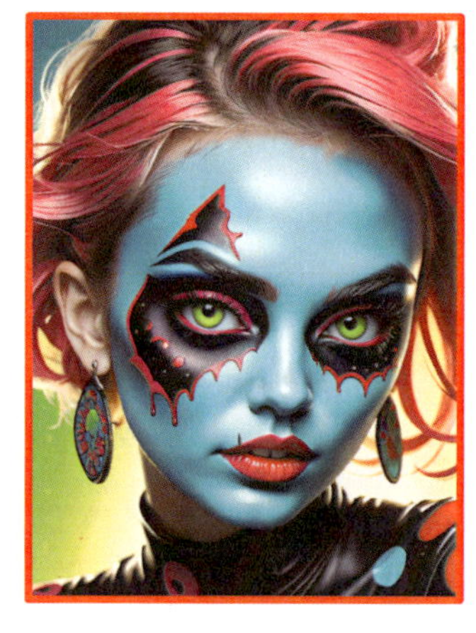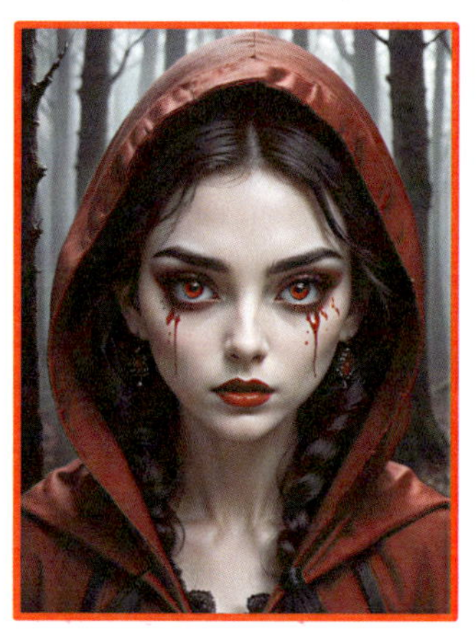
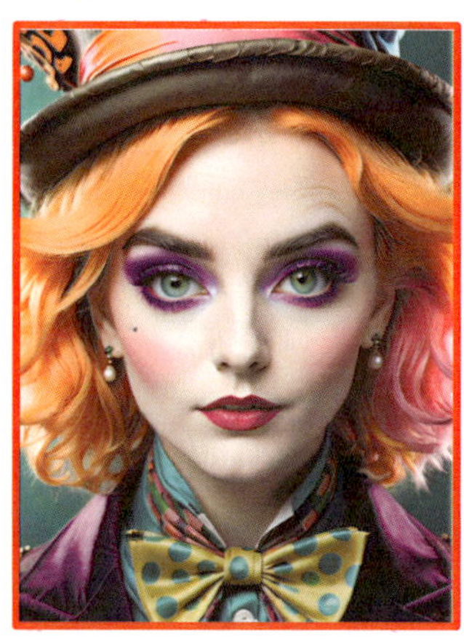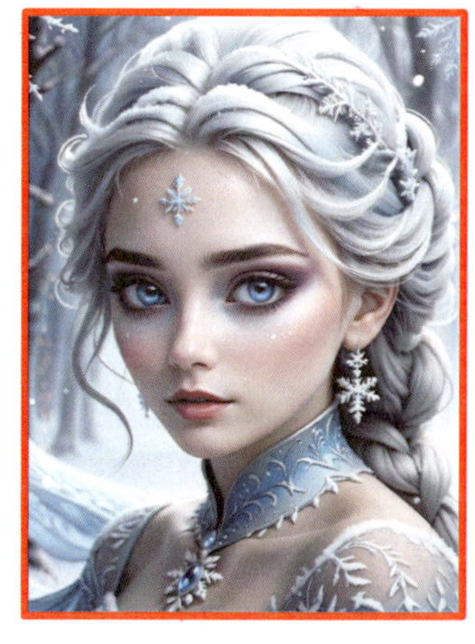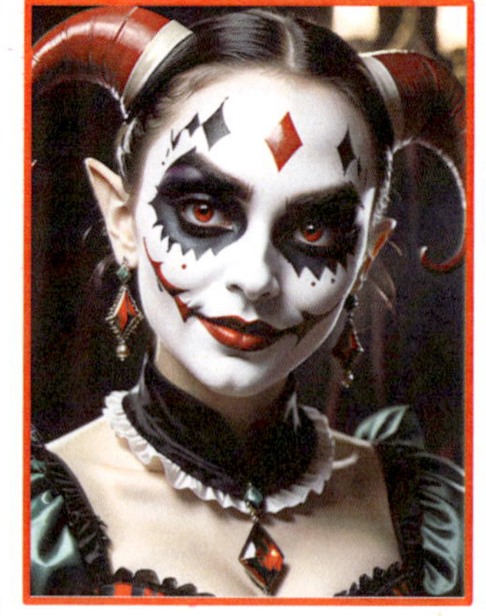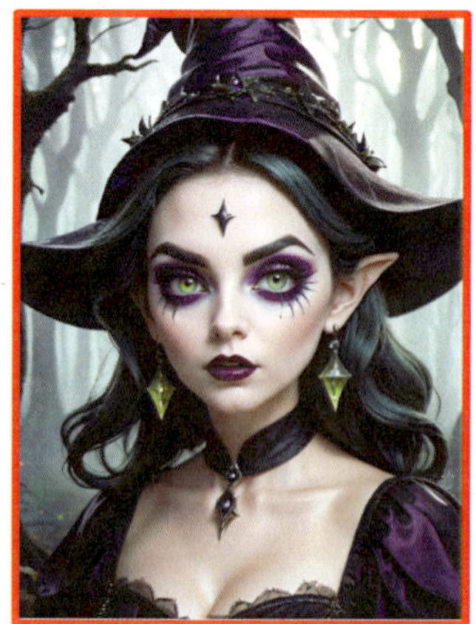

INTRODUCTION TO THE BOOK

WELCOME TO THE WORLD OF HALLOWEEN MAKEUP, WHERE EVERY FACE BECOMES A CANVAS, AND EVERY CREATION TELLS A STORY.

THIS BOOK IS DESIGNED FOR ALL HALLOWEEN ENTHUSIASTS, FROM THOSE JUST BEGINNING THEIR MAKEUP JOURNEY TO THOSE LOOKING TO REFINE THEIR SKILLS. OUR DETAILED STEP-BY-STEP INSTRUCTIONS WILL GUIDE YOU THROUGH THE PROCESS OF CREATING STUNNING, DARK, AND UNIQUE LOOKS THAT WILL CAPTIVATE YOUR FRIENDS AND FAMILY.

EACH STYLE IN THIS BOOK HAS BEEN CRAFTED TO BE BOTH VISUALLY STRIKING AND EASY TO RECREATE. WHETHER YOU WANT TO BECOME A DARK WITCH, A DEVILISH JESTER, OR AN ICY QUEEN, YOU'LL FIND SOMETHING HERE TO INSPIRE YOU. OUR INSPIRATIONS DRAW FROM VARIOUS CULTURES, MYTHS, AND LEGENDS TO CREATE UNFORGETTABLE LOOKS FOR THE SPOOKIEST NIGHT OF THE YEAR.

REMEMBER, MAKEUP IS NOT JUST A WAY TO CHANGE YOUR APPEARANCE — IT'S AN ART FORM THAT ALLOWS YOU TO EXPRESS YOURSELF, STEP INTO ANOTHER ROLE, AND CREATE A ONE-OF-A-KIND ATMOSPHERE. WITH EACH BRUSHSTROKE, WITH EVERY APPLIED COLOR, YOU ARE CREATING SOMETHING EXTRAORDINARY. OUR GUIDES WILL LEAD YOU THROUGH EACH STEP, BUT THE FINAL INTERPRETATION IS YOURS TO MAKE.

DON'T FORGET TO TAKE CARE OF YOUR HEALTH AND SAFETY WHILE CREATING YOUR MAKEUP MASTERPIECES BY FOLLOWING THE BHP (HEALTH AND SAFETY) GUIDELINES PROVIDED BELOW. ENJOY THE CREATIVE PROCESS AND HAVE FUN EXPLORING THE MAGIC OF HALLOWEEN!

HEALTH AND SAFETY GUIDELINES FOR MAKEUP APPLICATION

CLEAN HANDS:

ALWAYS WASH YOUR HANDS BEFORE AND AFTER APPLYING MAKEUP. CLEAN HANDS PREVENT THE TRANSFER OF BACTERIA TO YOUR SKIN AND MAKEUP PRODUCTS, MINIMIZING THE RISK OF INFECTIONS.

TOOL HYGIENE:

ENSURE THAT ALL MAKEUP TOOLS, SUCH AS BRUSHES, SPONGES, AND APPLICATORS, ARE CLEAN BEFORE USE. REGULARLY WASH YOUR BRUSHES AND REPLACE SPONGES TO AVOID THE BUILDUP OF BACTERIA AND COSMETIC RESIDUE.

PRODUCT TESTING:

BEFORE APPLYING NEW COSMETICS TO YOUR FACE, CONDUCT AN ALLERGY TEST. APPLY A SMALL AMOUNT OF THE PRODUCT ON THE INSIDE OF YOUR WRIST OR BEHIND YOUR EAR AND WAIT 24 HOURS TO ENSURE IT DOESN'T CAUSE AN ALLERGIC REACTION.

AVOID CONTACT WITH EYES:

WHEN APPLYING COSMETICS AROUND THE EYES, BE ESPECIALLY CAREFUL. AVOID GETTING MAKEUP INTO YOUR EYES TO PREVENT IRRITATION OR DAMAGE.

SAFE STORAGE OF COSMETICS:

STORE COSMETICS IN A COOL, DRY PLACE AWAY FROM DIRECT SUNLIGHT. ENSURE THEY ARE TIGHTLY SEALED TO AVOID CONTAMINATION AND EXTEND THEIR SHELF LIFE.

EXPIRATION DATES:

PAY ATTENTION TO THE EXPIRATION DATES OF COSMETICS. DO NOT USE PRODUCTS BEYOND THEIR EXPIRATION DATE, AS THEY MAY LOSE THEIR EFFECTIVENESS OR BECOME UNSAFE FOR YOUR SKIN.

SKIN REST:

AFTER THE EVENT OR PHOTO SESSION, REMEMBER TO THOROUGHLY CLEANSE YOUR FACE OF ALL MAKEUP PRODUCTS. ALLOW YOUR SKIN TO BREATHE AND REJUVENATE BY APPLYING A MOISTURIZING CREAM.

AVOID SHARING COSMETICS:

MAKEUP PRODUCTS SUCH AS LIPSTICKS, MASCARAS, AND FOUNDATIONS ARE MEANT FOR PERSONAL USE. SHARING THEM CAN LEAD TO THE SPREAD OF BACTERIA AND VIRUSES.

USE SAFE PRODUCTS:

MAKE SURE ALL THE COSMETICS YOU USE ARE SAFE FOR SKIN APPLICATION AND HAVE THE APPROPRIATE SAFETY CERTIFICATIONS. AVOID PRODUCTS CONTAINING INGREDIENTS TO WHICH YOU ARE ALLERGIC.

FOLLOWING THESE HEALTH AND SAFETY GUIDELINES WILL HELP YOU ENJOY CREATING MAKEUP LOOKS IN A SAFE AND HYGIENIC MANNER, ENSURING THE BEST RESULTS WITHOUT COMPROMISING YOUR HEALTH. CREATE, EXPERIMENT, AND HAVE FUN, ALL WHILE STAYING SAFE!

"VAMPIRE QUEEN"

STEP-BY-STEP INSTRUCTIONS:

1. SKIN PREPARATION:

TOOLS: FOUNDATION, CONCEALER, TRANSLUCENT POWDER.

INSTRUCTIONS: START BY APPLYING A LIGHT FOUNDATION ALL OVER THE FACE TO EVEN OUT THE SKIN TONE. THEN, USE CONCEALER UNDER THE EYES AND IN ANY AREAS THAT NEED EXTRA COVERAGE. FINISH WITH A TRANSLUCENT POWDER TO MATTIFY THE SKIN AND PROLONG THE MAKEUP'S WEAR.

2. CONTOURING THE FACE:

TOOLS: CONTOUR POWDER (COOL BROWN), CONTOURING BRUSH.

INSTRUCTIONS: CONTOUR THE FACE TO GIVE IT A MORE DEFINED AND GOTHIC LOOK. FOCUS ON THE CHEEKBONES, JAWLINE, AND SIDES OF THE NOSE USING A COOL-TONED BROWN SHADE.

3. EYES:

TOOLS: EYESHADOWS (BLACK, RED), EYELINER, MASCARA, FALSE LASHES (OPTIONAL).

INSTRUCTIONS: APPLY BLACK EYESHADOW OVER THE ENTIRE EYELID, BLENDING IT UPWARDS TOWARDS THE BROW. THEN, ADD RED EYESHADOW IN THE MIDDLE OF THE LID, BLENDING IT WITH THE BLACK. USE EYELINER TO CREATE A BOLD LINE, SLIGHTLY EXTENDED BEYOND THE OUTER CORNER OF THE EYE. ALSO, APPLY BLACK EYESHADOW ON THE LOWER LID TO DEFINE THE EYE. APPLY MASCARA AND OPTIONALLY FALSE LASHES FOR ADDED DRAMA.

4. BLOODY TEARS:

TOOLS: RED FACE PAINT OR RED EYELINER.

INSTRUCTIONS: USE A FINE BRUSH TO DRAW BLOODY TEARS FLOWING FROM THE LOWER LASH LINE. THE BLOOD SHOULD DRIP DOWN IN THIN STREAMS FOR A REALISTIC EFFECT.

5. LIPS:

TOOLS: RED LIPSTICK, BLACK EYELINER.

INSTRUCTIONS: APPLY INTENSELY RED LIPSTICK, MAKING SURE TO ACHIEVE A PERFECTLY SHAPED OUTLINE. YOU CAN ADD A TOUCH OF BLACK EYELINER TO THE CENTER OF THE LIPS FOR ADDED DEPTH AND A DRAMATIC EFFECT.

6. FINISHING TOUCHES:

TOOLS: HAIRSPRAY (OPTIONAL), RED CONTACT LENSES (OPTIONAL).

INSTRUCTIONS: IF DESIRED, USE RED CONTACT LENSES FOR AN INTENSELY VAMPIRIC LOOK. YOU CAN ALSO USE HAIRSPRAY TO HOLD THE HAIRSTYLE IN PLACE.

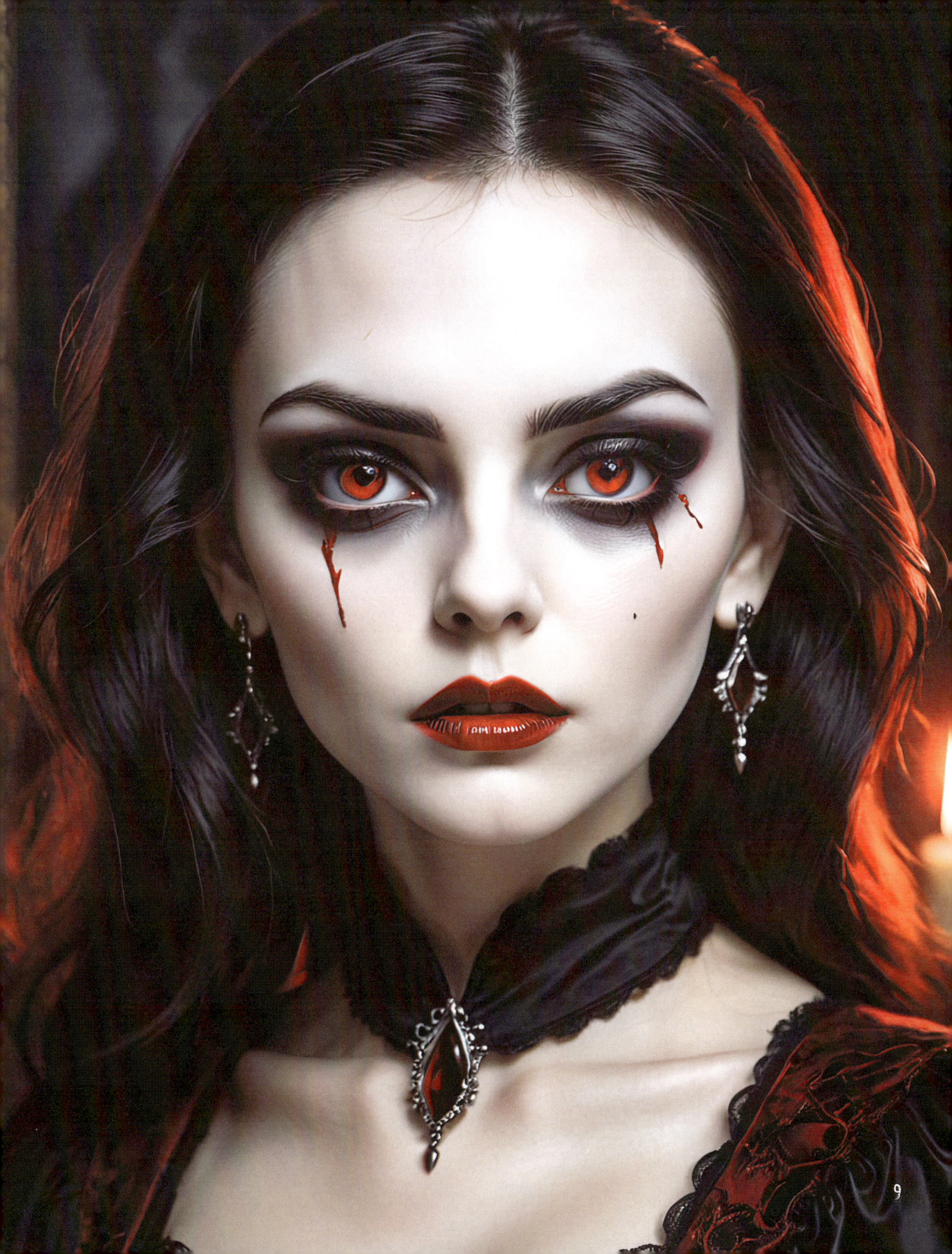

"SPIDER QUEEN"

STEP-BY-STEP INSTRUCTIONS:

1. SKIN PREPARATION:

TOOLS: FOUNDATION, CONCEALER, TRANSLUCENT POWDER.

INSTRUCTIONS: APPLY FOUNDATION EVENLY OVER THE FACE TO SMOOTH OUT SKIN TONE. USE CONCEALER TO COVER ANY IMPERFECTIONS. FINISH WITH A TRANSLUCENT POWDER TO MATTIFY THE FACE AND PROLONG THE MAKEUP'S WEAR.

2. CONTOURING THE FACE:

TOOLS: CONTOUR POWDER (COOL BROWN), CONTOURING BRUSH.

INSTRUCTIONS: GENTLY CONTOUR THE FACE, FOCUSING ON THE CHEEKBONES, JAWLINE, AND NOSE, TO ADD DEFINITION AND DEPTH.

3. EYES:

TOOLS: EYESHADOWS (BLACK), EYELINER, MASCARA, FALSE LASHES (OPTIONAL).

INSTRUCTIONS: APPLY BLACK EYESHADOW OVER THE ENTIRE EYELID, BLENDING UPWARDS TOWARD THE BROWS. THE SHADOW SHOULD BE INTENSE, ESPECIALLY AT THE OUTER CORNERS OF THE EYES. USE EYELINER TO CREATE A DRAMATIC SHAPE, EXTENDING THE LINE BEYOND THE OUTER CORNER OF THE EYE. LINE THE LOWER LASH LINE WITH BLACK EYESHADOW AS WELL. APPLY MASCARA AND OPTIONALLY FALSE LASHES TO ENHANCE THE EFFECT.

4. SPIDERWEB AND DECORATIONS:

TOOLS: BLACK FACE PAINT, FINE BRUSH, LASH GLUE (OPTIONAL), SPIDER-SHAPED DECORATION (OPTIONAL).

INSTRUCTIONS: USE A FINE BRUSH AND BLACK FACE PAINT TO DRAW A SPIDERWEB PATTERN ON THE FOREHEAD AND AROUND THE EYES. FOCUS ON SYMMETRICAL PLACEMENT OF THE LINES FOR A COHESIVE AND REALISTIC DESIGN. YOU CAN ALSO APPLY A SPIDER-SHAPED DECORATION ON THE CENTER OF THE FOREHEAD USING LASH GLUE.

5. LIPS:

TOOLS: RED LIPSTICK, LIP LINER.

INSTRUCTIONS: APPLY INTENSE RED LIPSTICK, CAREFULLY OUTLINING THE SHAPE OF THE LIPS. YOU CAN USE LIP LINER TO ENHANCE THE COLOR AND PRECISION OF THE MAKEUP.

6. FINISHING TOUCHES:

TOOLS: HAIRSPRAY (OPTIONAL), RED CONTACT LENSES (OPTIONAL).

INSTRUCTIONS: FOR A FULL EFFECT, CONSIDER ADDING RED CONTACT LENSES AND SETTING THE HAIRSTYLE WITH HAIRSPRAY.

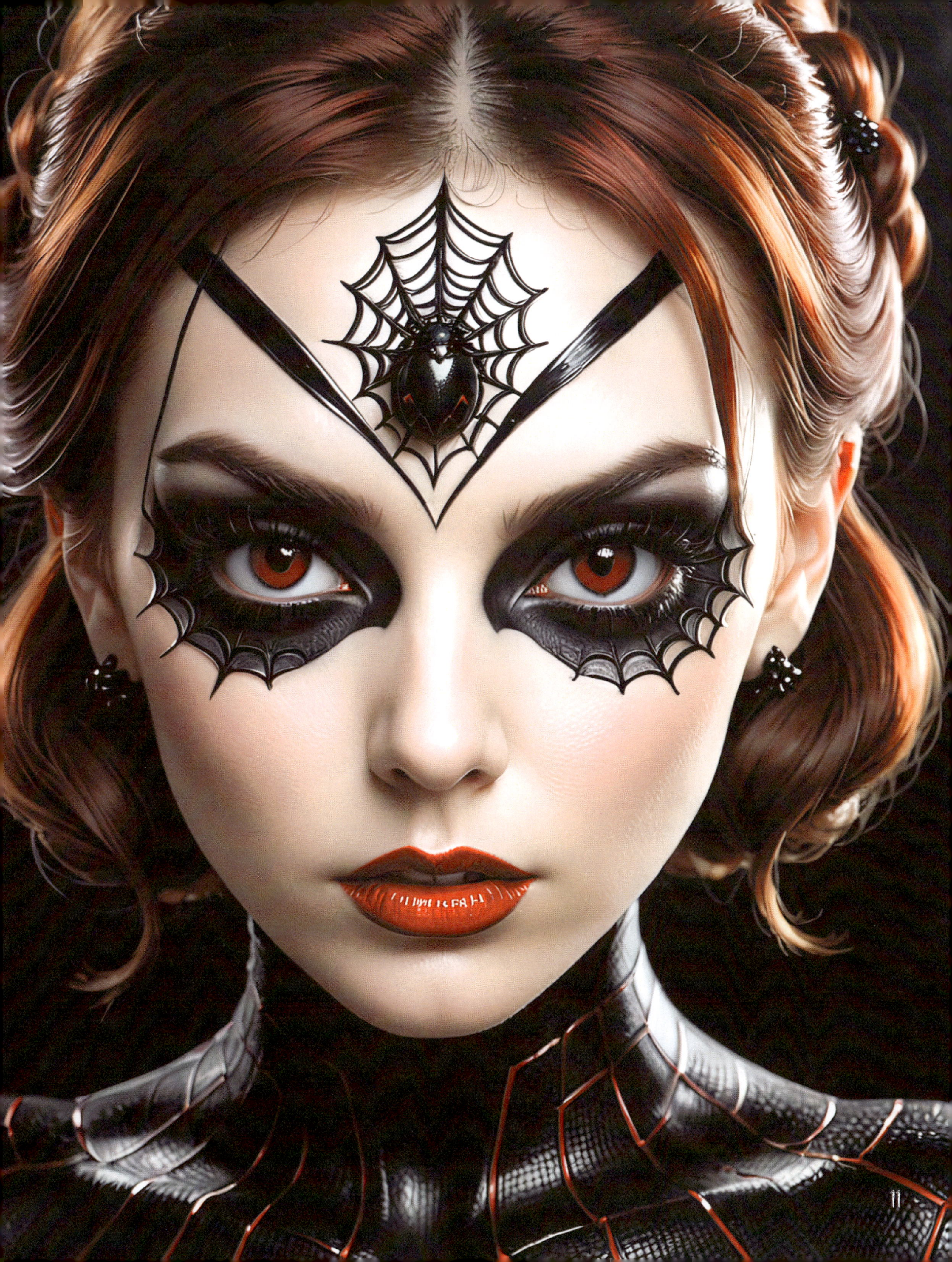

"ZOMBIE AWAKENING"

STEP-BY-STEP INSTRUCTIONS:

1. SKIN PREPARATION:

TOOLS: WHITE FACE PAINT, FOUNDATION, TRANSLUCENT POWDER.

INSTRUCTIONS: APPLY WHITE FACE PAINT AS A BASE TO ACHIEVE A PALE, DEAD LOOK. COVER THE ENTIRE FACE, NECK, AND ANY EXPOSED SKIN. YOU CAN ALSO USE A VERY LIGHT FOUNDATION FOR A MORE SUBTLE EFFECT. FINISH WITH A TRANSLUCENT POWDER TO SET THE PAINT.

2. CONTOURING THE FACE:

TOOLS: GRAY EYESHADOW, CONTOURING BRUSH.

INSTRUCTIONS: USE GRAY EYESHADOW TO ACCENTUATE THE NATURAL HOLLOWS OF THE FACE, SUCH AS THE CHEEKBONES, TEMPLES, AND JAWLINE. ALSO, CONTOUR AROUND THE EYES TO CREATE A SUNKEN, DEAD APPEARANCE.

3. EYES:

TOOLS: BLACK FACE PAINT OR EYELINER, BLACK EYESHADOW, MASCARA.

INSTRUCTIONS: APPLY BLACK FACE PAINT OR EYELINER AROUND THE EYES TO CREATE AN INTENSELY DARK BORDER. THEN, APPLY BLACK EYESHADOW ON THE EYELIDS, BLENDING UPWARDS TOWARDS THE BROWS. ALSO, USE BLACK SHADOW ON THE LOWER LASH LINE. APPLY MASCARA TO ENHANCE THE LASHES, GIVING THE EYES DEPTH AND A HAUNTING LOOK.

4. WOUNDS AND SCARS:

TOOLS: FAKE BLOOD, LATEX, FACE PAINTS (RED, BLACK).

INSTRUCTIONS: USE LATEX TO CREATE IRREGULAR TEXTURES ON THE SKIN, MIMICKING TORN FLESH. APPLY IT TO THE FOREHEAD, CHEEKS, AND OTHER SELECTED AREAS. ONCE DRY, PAINT THESE AREAS WITH BLACK AND RED FACE PAINTS TO SIMULATE DEEP, BLOODY WOUNDS. ADDITIONALLY, ADD FAKE BLOOD, LETTING IT DRIP FROM THE WOUNDS FOR A REALISTIC EFFECT.

5. LIPS:

TOOLS: RED AND BLACK LIPSTICK, FAKE BLOOD.

INSTRUCTIONS: APPLY RED LIPSTICK, THEN ADD SOME BLACK LIPSTICK TO THE CENTER FOR A LIFELESS EFFECT. YOU CAN ALSO ADD FAKE BLOOD AROUND THE MOUTH TO SIMULATE BLOODSTAINS.

6. FINISHING TOUCHES:

TOOLS: YELLOW CONTACT LENSES (OPTIONAL), HAIRSPRAY (OPTIONAL).

INSTRUCTIONS: FOR A COMPLETE EFFECT, CONSIDER WEARING YELLOW CONTACT LENSES TO INTENSIFY THE GAZE. THE HAIRSTYLE CAN BE SET WITH HAIRSPRAY TO MAKE IT LOOK MESSY AND DISHEVELED.

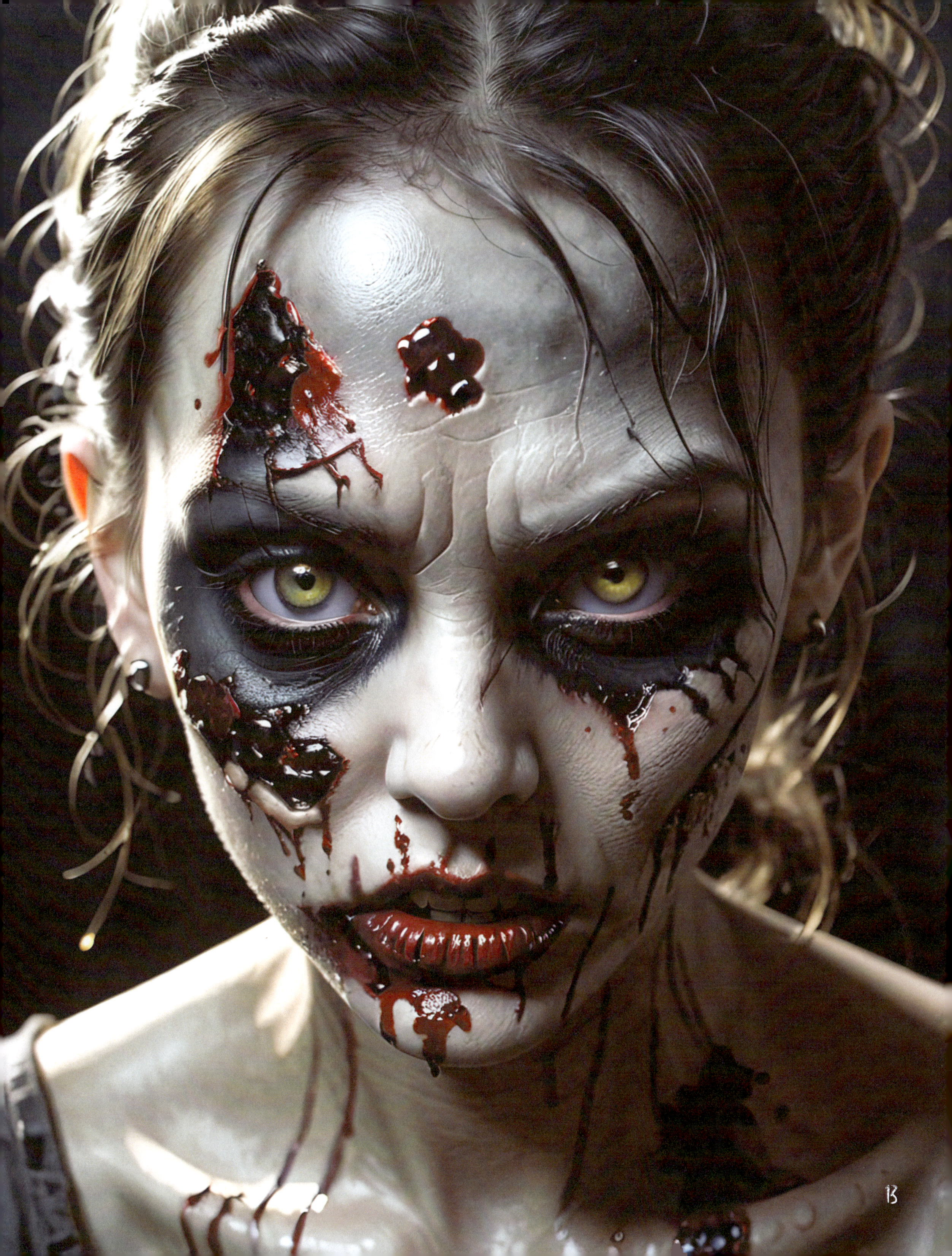

"CATRINA - DAY OF THE DEAD"

STEP-BY-STEP INSTRUCTIONS:

1. SKIN PREPARATION:

TOOLS: WHITE FACE PAINT, BRUSH OR SPONGE FOR APPLICATION.

INSTRUCTIONS: APPLY WHITE FACE PAINT ALL OVER THE FACE TO CREATE A SMOOTH AND EVEN BASE. ENSURE THE PAINT IS EVENLY DISTRIBUTED, INCLUDING ON THE EYELIDS AND LIPS.

2. EYES:

TOOLS: BLUE AND BLACK EYESHADOWS, EYELINER, BLENDING BRUSH.

INSTRUCTIONS: USE BLUE EYESHADOW, APPLYING IT AROUND THE ENTIRE EYE AREA TO CREATE LARGE, ROUND SHAPES RESEMBLING EYE SOCKETS. THEN, USE BLACK EYESHADOW TO ACCENTUATE THE CONTOURS AND ADD DEPTH. OUTLINE THE EDGES OF THESE CIRCLES WITH EYELINER FOR A BOLD LOOK.

3. NOSE:

TOOLS: BLACK FACE PAINT OR EYELINER.

INSTRUCTIONS: APPLY BLACK PAINT TO THE TIP OF THE NOSE, CREATING AN INVERTED HEART SHAPE TO SIMULATE A SKULL'S HOLLOW NOSE.

4. DETAILS:

TOOLS: BLACK AND COLORFUL FACE PAINTS, FINE BRUSH.

INSTRUCTIONS: WITH BLACK FACE PAINT, DRAW DELICATE LINES EXTENDING FROM THE CORNERS OF THE MOUTH, RESEMBLING THE STITCHES OF A SKULL. ADD DECORATIVE PATTERNS AROUND THE EYES, ON THE FOREHEAD, AND ON THE CHIN USING VIBRANT COLORS LIKE RED, BLUE, AND ORANGE. THE DESIGNS CAN REFERENCE FLORAL MOTIFS TYPICAL OF THE CATRINA STYLE.

5. LIPS:

TOOLS: RED LIPSTICK, BLACK EYELINER.

INSTRUCTIONS: APPLY RED LIPSTICK, CAREFULLY OUTLINING THE SHAPE OF THE LIPS. USE EYELINER TO OUTLINE THE LIPS AND THEN EXTEND THE LINE AT THE SIDES TO CREATE AN EFFECT OF ELONGATED MOUTH.

6. FINISHING TOUCHES:

TOOLS: COLORFUL FLOWERS FOR HAIR, EARRINGS, NECKLACE.

INSTRUCTIONS: COMPLETE THE LOOK BY ADDING COLORFUL FLOWERS TO THE HAIR, ALONG WITH MATCHING EARRINGS AND A NECKLACE TO EMPHASIZE THE DAY OF THE DEAD INSPIRED STYLE.

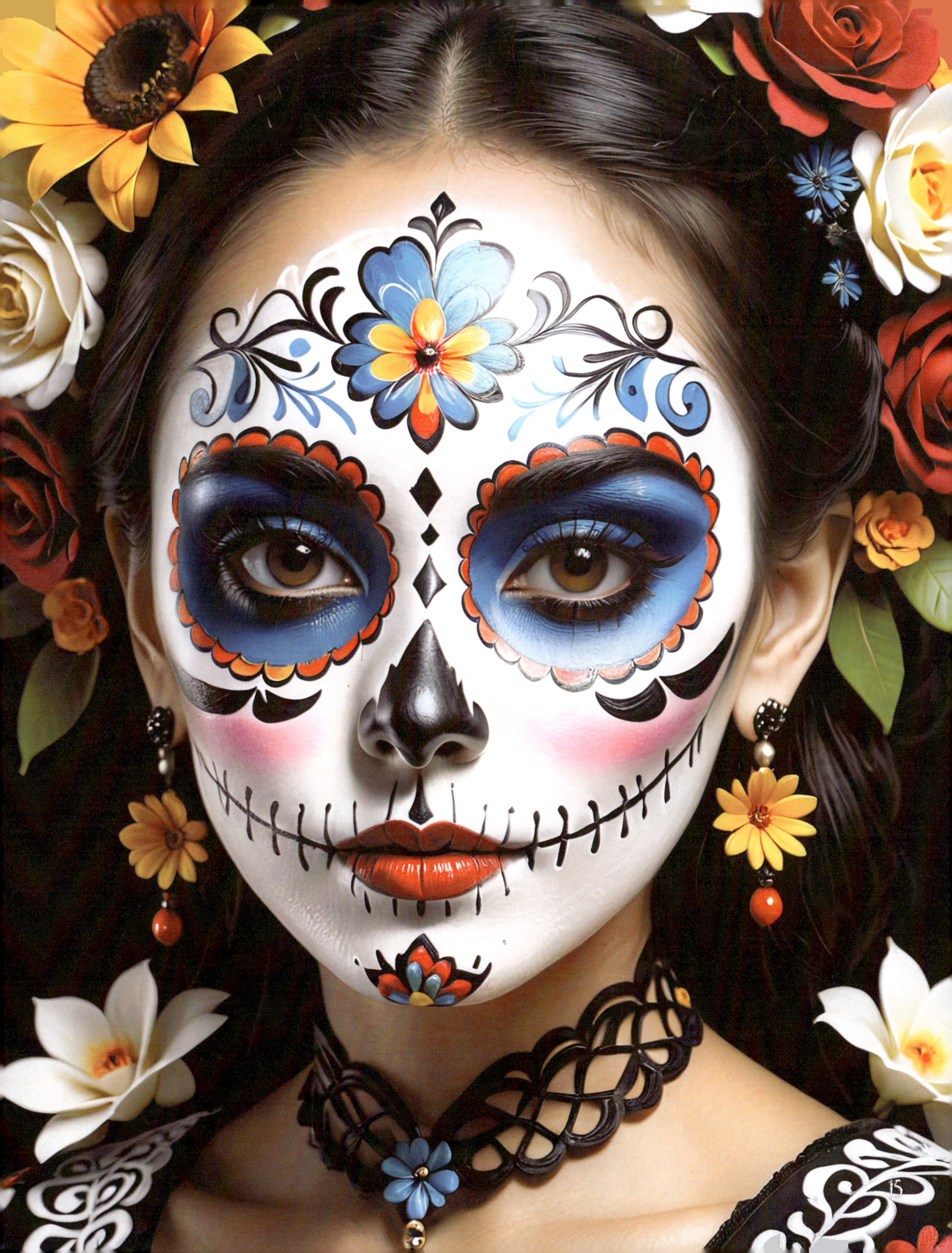

"DARK WITCH"

STEP-BY-STEP INSTRUCTIONS:

1. SKIN PREPARATION:

TOOLS: GREEN FACE PAINT, BRUSH OR SPONGE FOR APPLICATION.

INSTRUCTIONS: APPLY GREEN FACE PAINT ALL OVER THE FACE TO ACHIEVE A UNIFORM, GREENISH COMPLEXION CHARACTERISTIC OF A DARK WITCH. ENSURE THE PAINT IS EVENLY DISTRIBUTED, INCLUDING ON THE NECK AND EARS.

2. EYES:

TOOLS: PURPLE AND BLACK EYESHADOWS, EYELINER, MASCARA.

INSTRUCTIONS: APPLY PURPLE EYESHADOW ON THE EYELIDS, BLENDING IT UPWARDS TOWARDS THE BROWS. USE BLACK EYESHADOW TO ACCENTUATE THE OUTER CORNERS OF THE EYES, ADDING DEPTH. DRAW A THIN LINE ON THE UPPER EYELID WITH EYELINER AND ALSO DEFINE THE LOWER LASH LINE. FINISH WITH MASCARA TO ENHANCE THE LASHES AND GIVE THE EYES INTENSITY.

3. EYEBROWS AND DETAILS:

TOOLS: BLACK FACE PAINT OR EYELINER, FINE BRUSH.

INSTRUCTIONS: USE BLACK FACE PAINT OR EYELINER TO ACCENTUATE THE EYEBROWS, GIVING THEM A SHARP, ARCHED SHAPE. ADD FINE, SPIDER-LIKE LINES EXTENDING FROM THE OUTER CORNERS OF THE EYES TO CREATE A CRACKED SKIN EFFECT.

4. LIPS:

TOOLS: PURPLE LIPSTICK, BLACK EYELINER.

INSTRUCTIONS: APPLY PURPLE LIPSTICK, CAREFULLY OUTLINING THE LIPS. FOR ADDED DRAMA, LIGHTLY OUTLINE THE LIPS WITH BLACK EYELINER.

5. FINISHING TOUCHES:

TOOLS: WITCH HAT, PURPLE ACCENT (E.G., SCARF), EARRINGS.

INSTRUCTIONS: COMPLETE THE MAKEUP BY WEARING A CHARACTERISTIC WITCH'S HAT AND ADDING PURPLE ACCESSORIES, SUCH AS A SCARF OR NECKLACE, TO ENHANCE THE DARK AND MYSTERIOUS APPEARANCE.

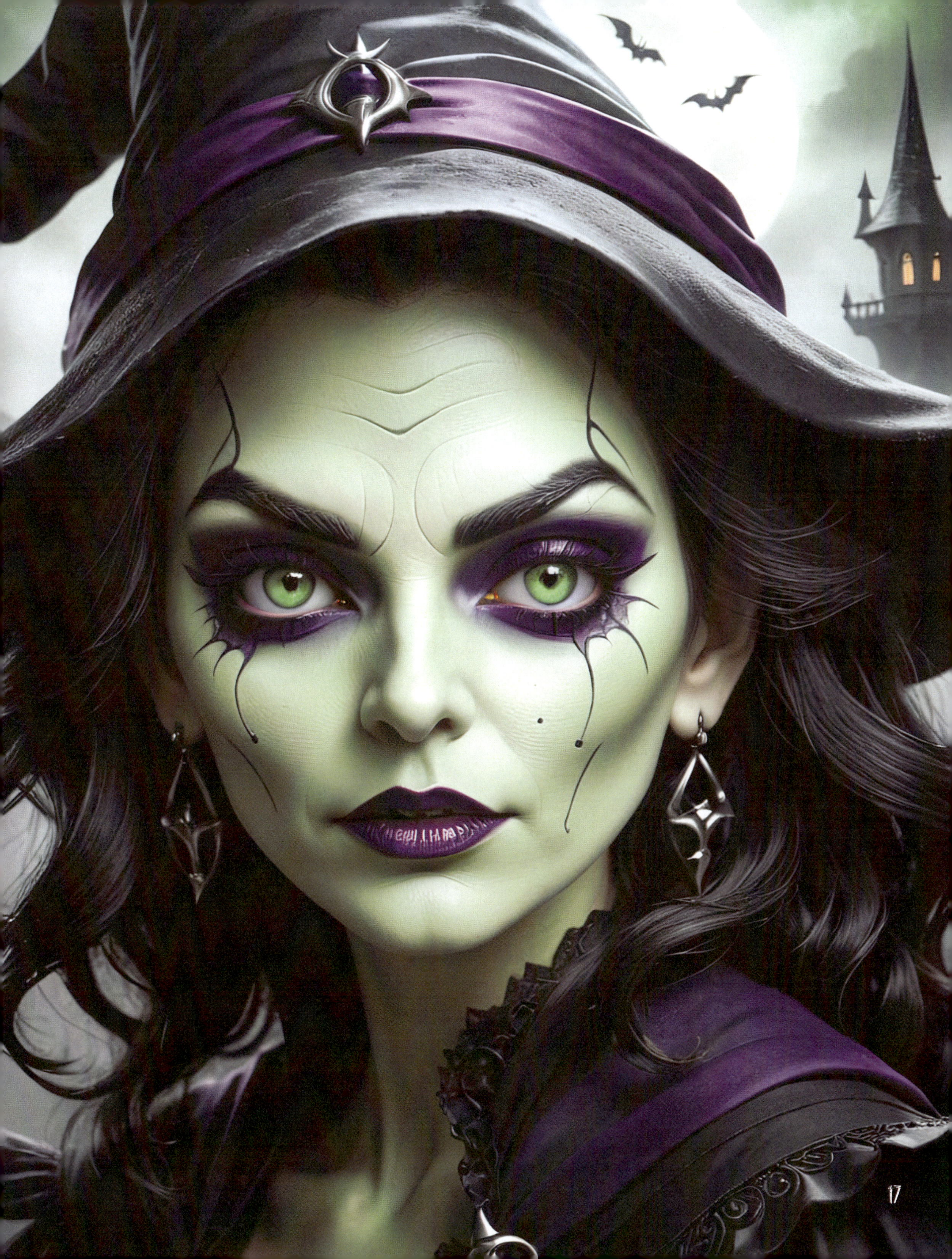

17

"SINISTER CLOWN"

STEP-BY-STEP INSTRUCTIONS:

1. SKIN PREPARATION:

TOOLS: WHITE FACE PAINT, BRUSH OR SPONGE FOR APPLICATION.

INSTRUCTIONS: APPLY WHITE FACE PAINT ALL OVER THE FACE TO CREATE A UNIFORM, WHITE BASE CHARACTERISTIC OF A CLOWN. ENSURE THE PAINT IS EVENLY DISTRIBUTED ACROSS THE ENTIRE FACE, INCLUDING THE EARS AND NECK.

2. EYES:

TOOLS: BLACK EYELINER, BLACK FACE PAINT, FINE BRUSH.

INSTRUCTIONS: USE BLACK EYELINER TO ACCENTUATE THE EYES, CREATING DRAMATIC LINES AROUND THE UPPER AND LOWER LASH LINES. THEN, WITH A FINE BRUSH, DRAW VERTICAL LINES EXTENDING FROM THE LOWER EYELID DOWNWARDS AND FROM THE UPPER EYELID UPWARDS, REACHING ALMOST TO THE EYEBROWS AND CHEEKS.

3. NOSE:

TOOLS: RED FACE PAINT OR CLOWN NOSE.

INSTRUCTIONS: APPLY RED PAINT TO THE TIP OF THE NOSE, FORMING THE CLASSIC ROUND CLOWN NOSE. ALTERNATIVELY, USE A FAKE RED CLOWN NOSE FOR ADDED REALISM.

4. LIPS:

TOOLS: RED LIPSTICK, BLACK FACE PAINT OR EYELINER.

INSTRUCTIONS: APPLY RED LIPSTICK TO THE LIPS, EXTENDING THE CORNERS BEYOND THE NATURAL LIP LINE TO CREATE A SINISTER SMILE. FOR ADDED DRAMA, USE BLACK PAINT OR EYELINER TO OUTLINE THE LIPS, CREATING A STARK CONTRAST.

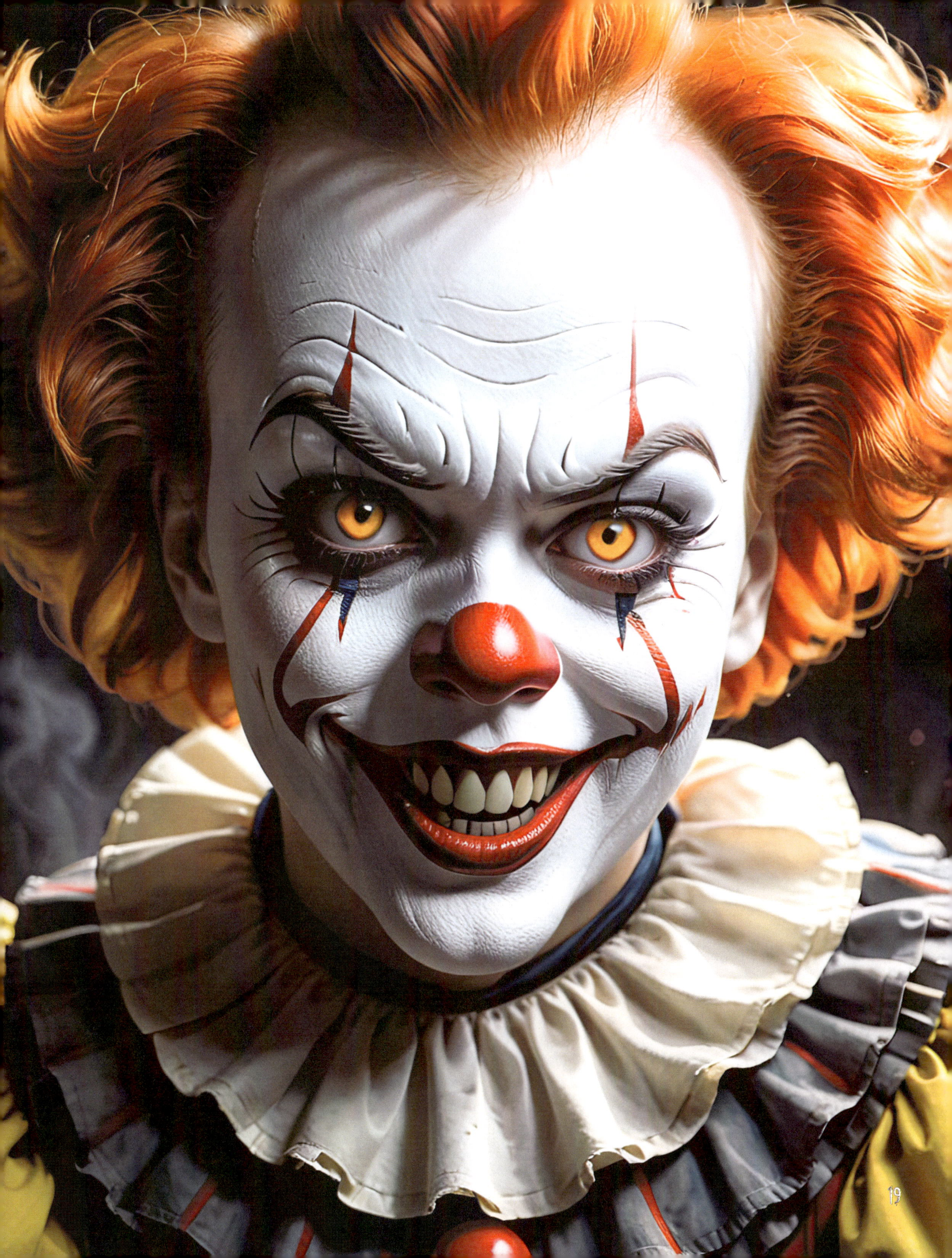

"DEMONIC QUEEN OF HELL"

STEP-BY-STEP INSTRUCTIONS:

1. SKIN PREPARATION:

TOOLS: WHITE FACE PAINT, BRUSH OR SPONGE FOR APPLICATION.

INSTRUCTIONS: APPLY WHITE FACE PAINT TO ACHIEVE A BRIGHT, ALMOST DEMONIC COMPLEXION. ENSURE THE PAINT IS EVENLY DISTRIBUTED, INCLUDING ON THE NECK AND EARS.

2. CONTOURING AND DEFINING FACIAL FEATURES:

TOOLS: BLACK FACE PAINT, CONTOURING BRUSH, FINE BRUSH.

INSTRUCTIONS: USE BLACK FACE PAINT TO ACCENTUATE AND OUTLINE SHARP FACIAL CONTOURS. FOCUS ON THE JAWLINE, TEMPLES, AND SIDES OF THE NOSE. ADD DEMONIC, SPIKED PATTERNS ON THE FOREHEAD, CHEEKS, AND AROUND THE EYES TO GIVE THE FACE A SINISTER EXPRESSION.

3. EYES:

TOOLS: RED AND BLACK EYESHADOWS, EYELINER, MASCARA.

INSTRUCTIONS: APPLY BLACK EYESHADOW ON THE EYELIDS, BLENDING IT UPWARDS AND TOWARDS THE OUTER CORNERS OF THE EYES. ADD RED EYESHADOW TO THE CENTER OF THE LIDS TO CREATE A FIERY EFFECT. USE EYELINER TO DEFINE THE LASH LINES AND ADD DEPTH TO THE EYES. FINISH WITH MASCARA TO ENHANCE THE LASHES.

4. NOSE:

TOOLS: BLACK FACE PAINT OR EYELINER.

INSTRUCTIONS: PAINT THE NOSE IN A SHARP, DEMONIC SHAPE TO EMPHASIZE THE SINISTER APPEARANCE.

5. LIPS:

TOOLS: RED LIPSTICK, BLACK FACE PAINT OR EYELINER.

INSTRUCTIONS: APPLY RED LIPSTICK TO THE LIPS, CREATING AN INTENSE, BLOOD-RED COLOR. FOR A MORE DRAMATIC EFFECT, OUTLINE THE LIPS WITH BLACK PAINT OR EYELINER TO CREATE SHARP EDGES.

6. HORNS AND DETAILS:

TOOLS: HORNS (FAKE OR LATEX-FORMED), SKIN ADHESIVE, ADDITIONAL ACCESSORIES (E.G., EARRINGS).

INSTRUCTIONS: ATTACH FAKE HORNS TO THE FOREHEAD USING SKIN ADHESIVE. ADDITIONALLY, YOU CAN ADD DECORATIVE EARRINGS OR OTHER ACCESSORIES TO COMPLETE THE DEMONIC LOOK.

7. FINISHING TOUCHES:

TOOLS: RED CONTACT LENSES (OPTIONAL), BODY PAINT IN BLACK AND RED TONES.

INSTRUCTIONS: FOR A FULL EFFECT, WEAR RED CONTACT LENSES TO INTENSIFY THE GAZE. PAINT THE NECK AND SHOULDERS WITH BLACK AND RED BODY PAINT TO COMPLETE THE DEMONIC APPEARANCE.

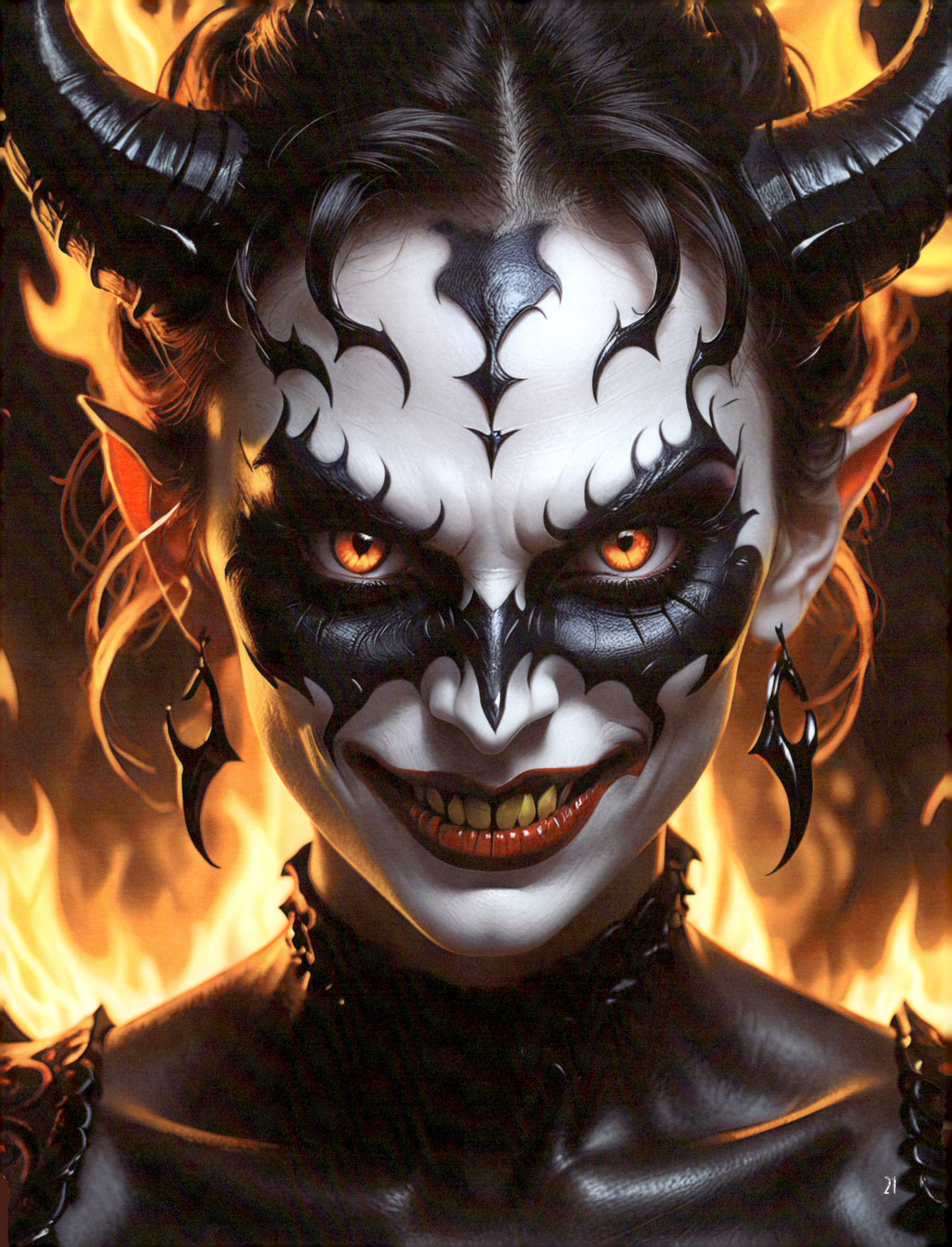

"PORCELAIN DOLL"

STEP-BY-STEP INSTRUCTIONS:

1. SKIN PREPARATION:

TOOLS: LIGHT FOUNDATION, TRANSLUCENT POWDER, BLUSH.

INSTRUCTIONS: APPLY LIGHT FOUNDATION ALL OVER THE FACE TO ACHIEVE A SMOOTH, PORCELAIN-LIKE COMPLEXION. ENSURE THE FOUNDATION IS EVENLY DISTRIBUTED, THEN SET IT WITH TRANSLUCENT POWDER TO GIVE THE SKIN A MATTE FINISH. APPLY PINK BLUSH ON THE APPLES OF THE CHEEKS TO CREATE A SOFT, DOLL-LIKE EFFECT.

2. EYES:

TOOLS: PINK EYESHADOW, BLACK EYELINER, FALSE LASHES, WHITE PENCIL.

INSTRUCTIONS: APPLY PINK EYESHADOW ON THE ENTIRE EYELID, BLENDING IT GENTLY UPWARDS. USE BLACK EYELINER TO DRAW A DEFINED LINE ON THE UPPER EYELID, SLIGHTLY EXTENDING IT TOWARDS THE OUTER CORNER. ON THE LOWER EYELID, DRAW A THIN LINE CLOSE TO THE LASH LINE, BUT HIGHLIGHT THE WATERLINE WITH A WHITE PENCIL TO MAKE THE EYES APPEAR LARGER. FINISH BY APPLYING FALSE LASHES TO ACHIEVE A BIG, DOLL-LIKE EYE EFFECT.

3. EYEBROWS:

TOOLS: BROW PENCIL IN A NATURAL SHADE.

INSTRUCTIONS: GENTLY DEFINE THE EYEBROWS, GIVING THEM A PERFECTLY ROUNDED SHAPE THAT ENHANCES THE DOLL-LIKE EXPRESSION. THE BROWS SHOULD BE SUBTLE AND HARMONIOUSLY BLEND WITH THE REST OF THE MAKEUP.

4. LIPS:

TOOLS: PINK LIPSTICK, LIP GLOSS.

INSTRUCTIONS: APPLY PINK LIPSTICK, CAREFULLY OUTLINING THE LIPS FOR A PERFECTLY DEFINED SHAPE. THE LIPS SHOULD APPEAR FULL AND SLIGHTLY ROUNDED. ADD A LAYER OF GLOSS TO THE CENTER OF THE LIPS FOR ADDED SHINE AND VOLUME.

5. DETAILS:

TOOLS: WHITE FACE PAINT OR EYELINER, BLUSH.

INSTRUCTIONS: USE WHITE PAINT OR EYELINER TO ADD SMALL DOTS OR ACCENTS ON THE CHEEKS TO EMPHASIZE THE PORCELAIN LOOK. YOU CAN ALSO APPLY AN EXTRA LAYER OF BLUSH TO INTENSIFY THE DOLL-LIKE EFFECT.

6. FINISHING TOUCHES:

TOOLS: PASTEL-COLORED WIG (E.G., PINK), ACCESSORIES (E.G., HEART-SHAPED EARRINGS).

INSTRUCTIONS: TO COMPLETE THE LOOK, WEAR A PASTEL-COLORED WIG, SUCH AS PINK, AND ADD ACCESSORIES LIKE HEART-SHAPED EARRINGS. STYLE THE HAIR IN SOFT WAVES TO ENHANCE THE DELICATE, DOLL-LIKE APPEARANCE.

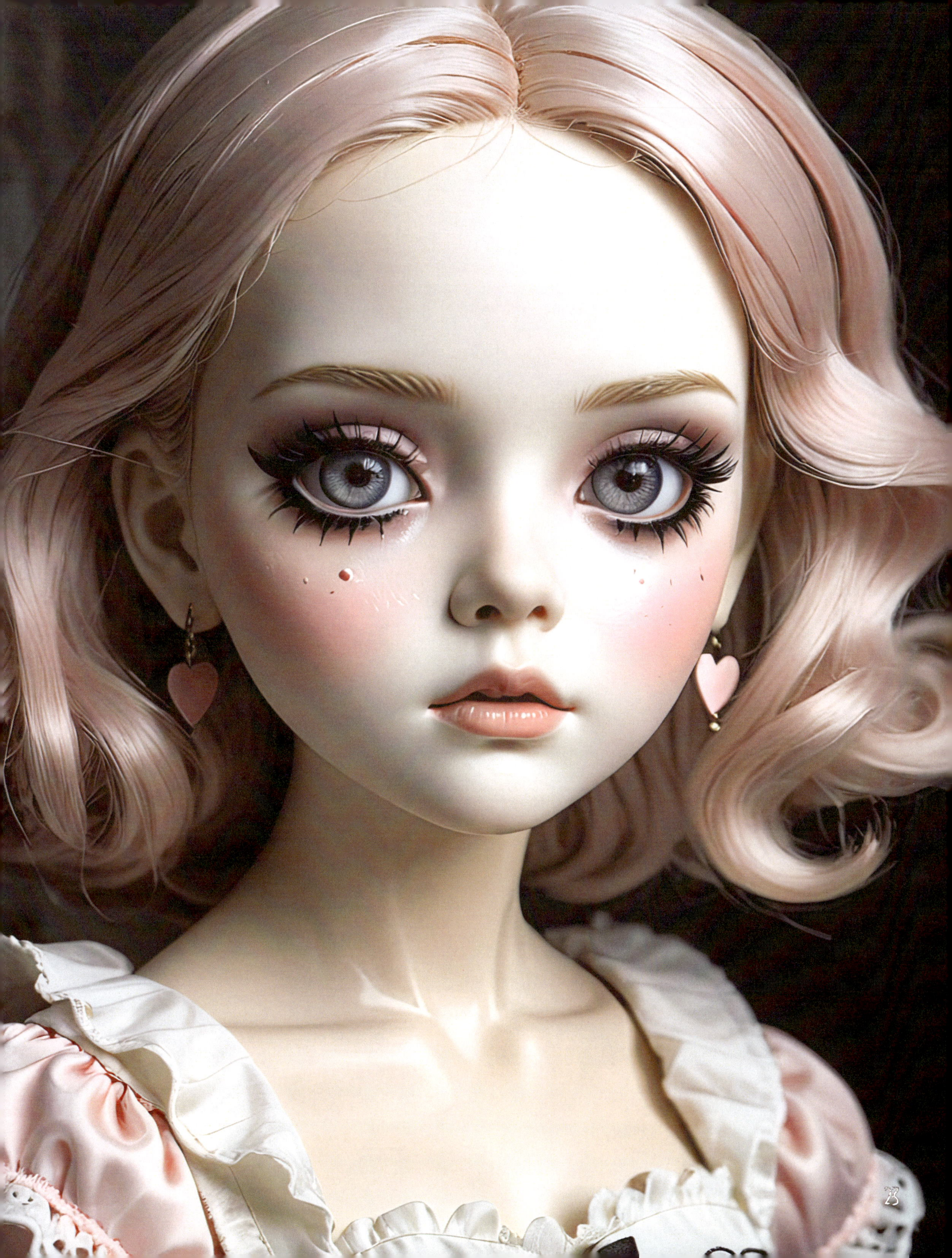

"WEREWOLF QUEEN"

STEP-BY-STEP INSTRUCTIONS:

1. SKIN PREPARATION:

TOOLS: WHITE FACE PAINT, BRUSH OR SPONGE FOR APPLICATION.

INSTRUCTIONS: APPLY WHITE FACE PAINT ALL OVER THE FACE TO ACHIEVE A BRIGHT, ALMOST ANIMALISTIC COMPLEXION. ENSURE THE PAINT IS EVENLY DISTRIBUTED, PARTICULARLY ON THE CHEEKS, NOSE, AND CHIN.

2. CONTOURING AND DEFINING FACIAL FEATURES:

TOOLS: GRAY AND BLACK EYESHADOWS, CONTOURING BRUSH.

INSTRUCTIONS: USE GRAY AND BLACK EYESHADOWS TO CONTOUR THE FACE, FOCUSING ON THE CHEEKS, TEMPLES, AND SIDES OF THE NOSE. CONTOUR THESE AREAS TO GIVE THE FACE A MORE WOLF-LIKE APPEARANCE.

3. EYES:

TOOLS: BLACK EYESHADOWS, EYELINER, MASCARA.

INSTRUCTIONS: APPLY BLACK EYESHADOW ON THE EYELIDS, BLENDING IT UPWARDS AND INTO THE OUTER CORNERS OF THE EYES TO CREATE A DEEP, MYSTERIOUS LOOK. USE EYELINER TO DRAW A DEFINED LINE ON THE UPPER AND LOWER LIDS, ACCENTUATING THE SHAPE OF THE EYES. FINISH WITH MASCARA TO ENHANCE THE LASHES AND ADD INTENSITY TO THE GAZE.

4. NOSE AND LIPS:

TOOLS: BLACK FACE PAINT, DARK BROWN LIPSTICK.

INSTRUCTIONS: PAINT THE TIP OF THE NOSE WITH BLACK FACE PAINT TO CREATE A WOLF-LIKE NOSE EFFECT. APPLY DARK BROWN LIPSTICK TO THE LIPS, GIVING THEM AN INTENSE, PREDATORY LOOK. YOU CAN ALSO USE BLACK FACE PAINT TO DRAW SUBTLE LINES EXTENDING FROM THE CORNERS OF THE MOUTH, ADDING A WILD TOUCH TO THE CHARACTER.

5. DETAILS:

TOOLS: BLACK FACE PAINT, FINE BRUSH.

INSTRUCTIONS: ADD DETAILS SUCH AS WOLF TEETH OR SPIKED PATTERNS AROUND THE EYES AND FOREHEAD TO ENHANCE THE ANIMALISTIC APPEARANCE. YOU CAN ALSO ADD SMALL LINES SIMULATING FUR ON THE EYEBROWS AND CHEEKS.

6. FINISHING TOUCHES:

TOOLS: WOLF EARS (FAKE OR LATEX-FORMED), FUR ACCESSORIES, EARRINGS.

INSTRUCTIONS: ATTACH FAKE WOLF EARS USING SKIN ADHESIVE AND ADD FUR ACCESSORIES TO COMPLETE THE WOLF-LIKE APPEARANCE. GOLD HOOP EARRINGS CAN ADD A TOUCH OF ELEGANCE WHILE EMPHASIZING THE WILD CHARACTER.

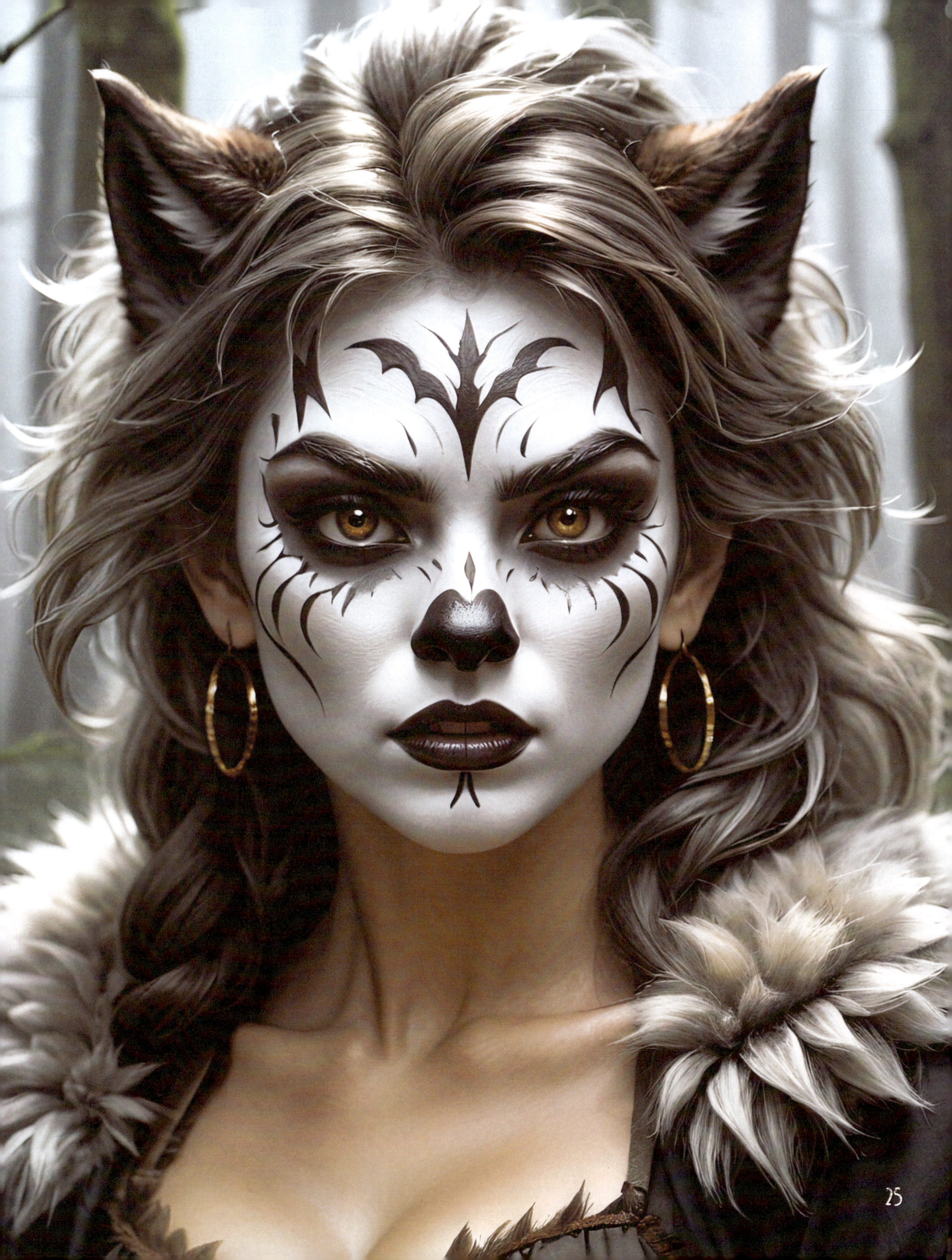

"DEEP SEA MERMAID"

STEP-BY-STEP INSTRUCTIONS:

1. SKIN PREPARATION:

TOOLS: COOL-TONED FOUNDATION, TRANSLUCENT POWDER.

INSTRUCTIONS: APPLY A COOL, SLIGHTLY PEARLESCENT FOUNDATION ALL OVER THE FACE TO ACHIEVE A SMOOTH, EVEN COMPLEXION. ENSURE THE FOUNDATION IS EVENLY BLENDED, THEN SET IT WITH TRANSLUCENT POWDER TO GIVE THE SKIN A LIGHT MATTE FINISH.

2. EYES:

TOOLS: BLUE, PURPLE, AND GREEN EYESHADOWS, EYELINER, MASCARA.

INSTRUCTIONS: APPLY BLUE EYESHADOW OVER THE ENTIRE EYELID, BLENDING IT GENTLY TOWARDS THE BROWS. ADD PURPLE EYESHADOW TO THE OUTER CORNERS OF THE EYES TO GIVE THE GAZE DEPTH. APPLY GREEN EYESHADOW ALONG THE LOWER EYELID TO HIGHLIGHT THE LOWER LASH LINE. USE EYELINER TO DRAW A THIN LINE ON THE UPPER EYELID AND ALSO SUBTLY DEFINE THE LOWER LASH LINE. FINISH WITH MASCARA TO ENHANCE THE EFFECT.

3. SCALES:

TOOLS: SCALE STENCIL (YOU CAN USE NETTING OR STENCILS), METALLIC EYESHADOWS IN SHADES OF TURQUOISE, GREEN, AND BLUE.

INSTRUCTIONS: PLACE THE SCALE STENCIL ON SELECTED AREAS OF THE FACE, SUCH AS THE FOREHEAD, CHEEKS, AND TEMPLES. GENTLY APPLY METALLIC EYESHADOWS TO CREATE THE FISH SCALE EFFECT. REMOVE THE STENCIL TO REVEAL A SYMMETRICAL PATTERN OF SCALES THAT WILL SHIMMER BEAUTIFULLY FROM DIFFERENT ANGLES.

4. LIPS:

TOOLS: PURPLE LIPSTICK, LIP GLOSS.

INSTRUCTIONS: APPLY PURPLE LIPSTICK TO THE LIPS, CAREFULLY OUTLINING THEIR SHAPE. ADD A TOUCH OF GLOSS TO THE CENTER OF THE LIPS FOR A SHINY EFFECT REMINISCENT OF GLISTENING SEAWATER.

5. DETAILS:

TOOLS: FAKE PEARLS, BODY ADHESIVE, FINE BRUSH.

INSTRUCTIONS: APPLY FAKE PEARLS TO SELECTED AREAS OF THE FACE, SUCH AS AROUND THE EYES OR ON THE FOREHEAD, TO ADD ELEGANCE AND A DEEP-SEA CHARACTER TO THE MAKEUP. USE BODY ADHESIVE TO SECURE THE PEARLS, ENSURING SYMMETRY.

6. FINISHING TOUCHES:

TOOLS: WIG IN SHADES OF PURPLE AND BLUE, ACCESSORIES (E.G., SHELL-SHAPED EARRINGS), GLITTER.

INSTRUCTIONS: WEAR A WIG IN SHADES OF PURPLE AND BLUE TO COMPLETE THE MERMAID LOOK. ADD ACCESSORIES LIKE SHELL-SHAPED EARRINGS AND GENTLY APPLY GLITTER TO THE HAIR AND SHOULDERS FOR A SHIMMERING WATER EFFECT.

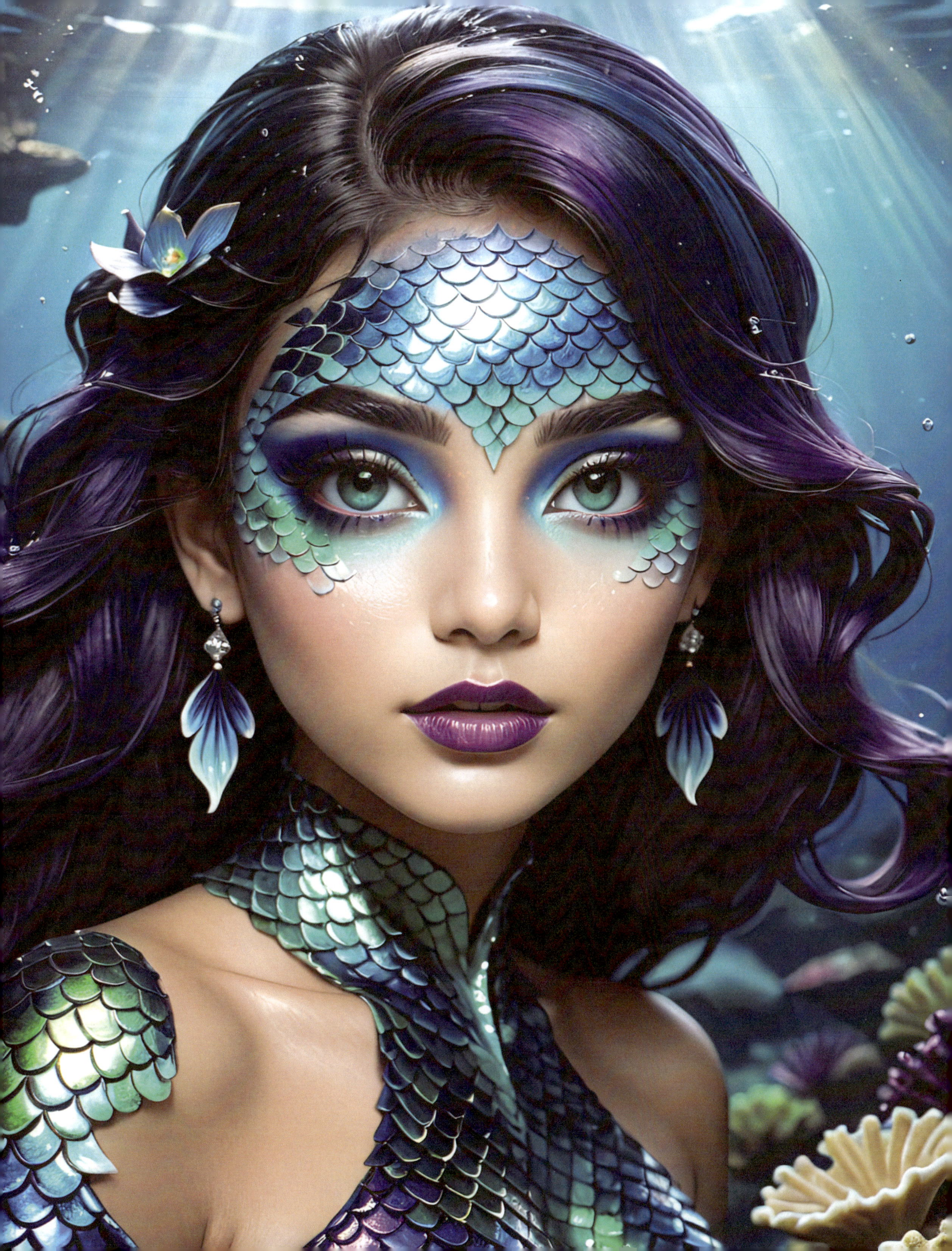

"COSMIC QUEEN"

STEP-BY-STEP INSTRUCTIONS:

1. SKIN PREPARATION:

TOOLS: GREEN-BLUE FACE PAINT, BRUSH OR SPONGE FOR APPLICATION.

INSTRUCTIONS: APPLY GREEN-BLUE FACE PAINT ALL OVER THE FACE TO ACHIEVE A UNIFORM, COSMIC SKIN TONE. ENSURE THE PAINT IS EVENLY BLENDED, CREATING A SMOOTH BASE FOR THE REST OF THE MAKEUP.

2. CONTOURING AND DEFINING FACIAL FEATURES:

TOOLS: PURPLE AND BLUE EYESHADOWS, CONTOURING BRUSH.

INSTRUCTIONS: USE PURPLE AND BLUE EYESHADOWS TO CONTOUR THE FACE, FOCUSING ON THE CHEEKS, TEMPLES, AND SIDES OF THE NOSE. ADD COLORS TO AREAS WHERE YOU WANT TO CREATE A COSMIC DEPTH AND MYSTERY.

3. EYES:

TOOLS: PURPLE AND GREEN EYESHADOWS, EYELINER, MASCARA.

INSTRUCTIONS: APPLY PURPLE EYESHADOW ON THE UPPER EYELIDS, BLENDING IT GENTLY TOWARDS THE BROWS. APPLY GREEN EYESHADOW ON THE LOWER EYELID TO HIGHLIGHT THE LOWER LASH LINE. USE EYELINER TO DRAW A DEFINED LINE ON THE UPPER LID. FINISH WITH MASCARA TO ENHANCE THE LASHES AND ADD DEPTH TO THE EYES.

4. COSMIC FOREHEAD DESIGN:

TOOLS: WHITE FACE PAINT, FINE BRUSH.

INSTRUCTIONS: USE WHITE PAINT TO CREATE A COSMIC DESIGN IN THE CENTER OF THE FOREHEAD. THE DESIGN CAN RESEMBLE A GALAXY, STARS, OR OTHER COSMIC MOTIFS, GIVING THE FACE A MYSTERIOUS, SPACE-LIKE APPEARANCE.

5. LIPS:

TOOLS: METALLIC PURPLE LIPSTICK, LIP GLOSS.

INSTRUCTIONS: APPLY METALLIC PURPLE LIPSTICK TO THE LIPS, CAREFULLY OUTLINING THEIR SHAPE. FOR AN ADDED EFFECT, APPLY GLOSS TO GIVE THE LIPS A SHINY, COSMIC GLOW.

6. DETAILS:

TOOLS: WHITE FACE PAINT, GLITTER, FINE BRUSH.

INSTRUCTIONS: ADD SMALL WHITE DOTS AND LINES ON THE CHEEKS AND AROUND THE EYES, RESEMBLING STARS AND CONSTELLATIONS. YOU CAN ALSO ADD GLITTER TO THE FACE AND NECKLINE FOR A SPARKLING STAR EFFECT.

7. FINISHING TOUCHES:

TOOLS: WIG OR HAIR DYE IN COSMIC SHADES (E.G., PURPLE, GREEN, BLUE), ACCESSORIES (E.G., COSMIC-THEMED EARRINGS).

INSTRUCTIONS: COMPLETE THE LOOK WITH A WIG OR HAIR DYE IN COSMIC SHADES TO TIE THE WHOLE LOOK TOGETHER. ADD COSMIC-THEMED EARRINGS TO EMPHASIZE THE GALACTIC APPEARANCE.

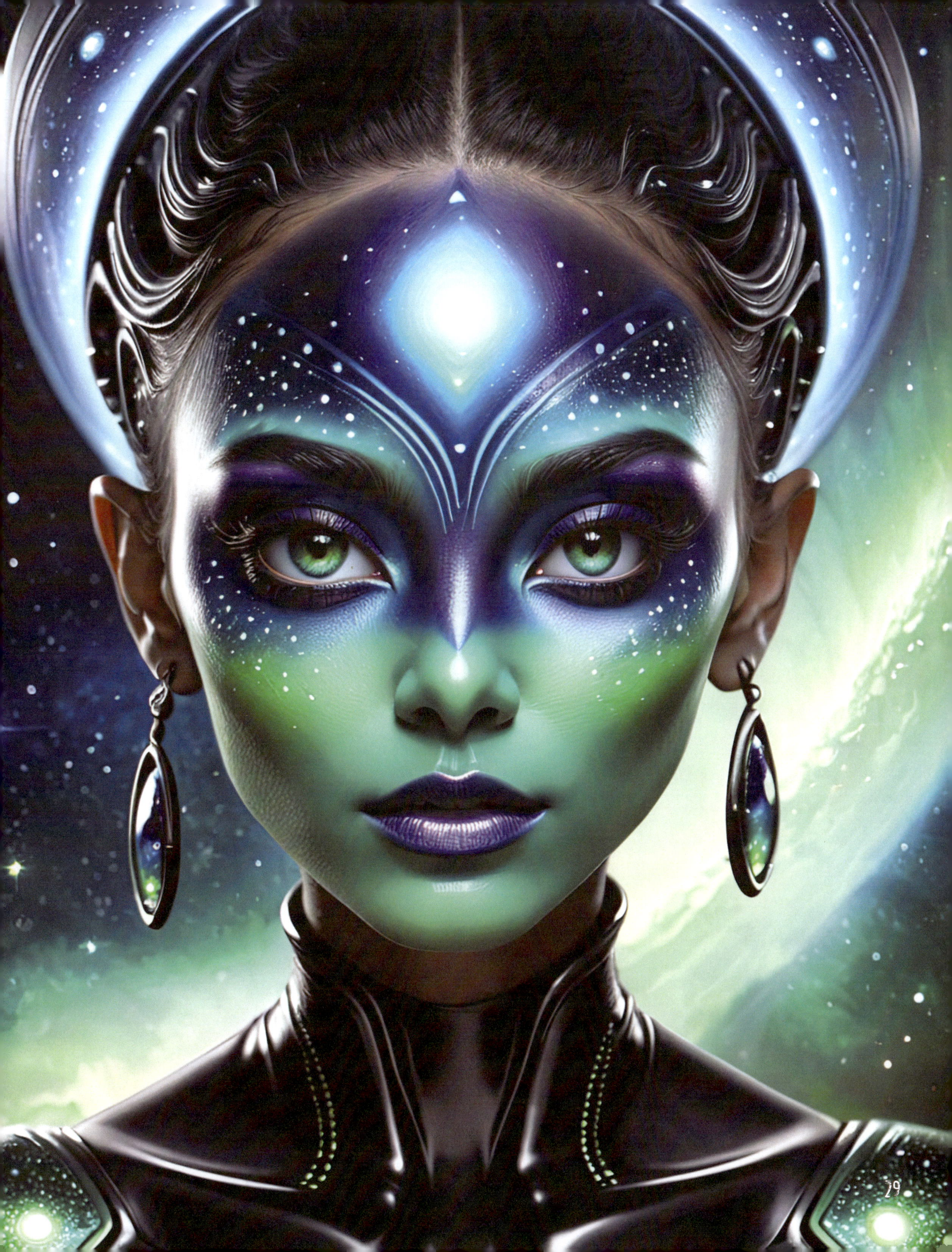

29

"AWAKENED ANCIENT MASK"

STEP-BY-STEP INSTRUCTIONS:

1. SKIN PREPARATION:

TOOLS: NATURAL-TONED FOUNDATION, TRANSLUCENT POWDER.

INSTRUCTIONS: APPLY FOUNDATION ALL OVER THE FACE TO ACHIEVE A SMOOTH, EVEN COMPLEXION. ENSURE THE FOUNDATION IS EVENLY BLENDED, THEN SET IT WITH TRANSLUCENT POWDER TO GIVE THE SKIN A LIGHT MATTE FINISH.

2. CREATING THE MASK EFFECT:

TOOLS: WHITE FACE PAINT, BEIGE FACE PAINT, FINE BRUSH, BLACK FACE PAINT.

INSTRUCTIONS: APPLY WHITE FACE PAINT TO SELECTED AREAS, CREATING THE OUTLINE OF AN ANCIENT MASK ON THE FOREHEAD, CHEEKS, AND CHIN. USE BEIGE FACE PAINT TO FILL IN THE CENTRAL PARTS OF THE MASK, CREATING AN AGED, CRACKED SURFACE EFFECT. USE A FINE BRUSH AND BLACK FACE PAINT TO ADD CRACKS AND DEPTH, CREATING THE ILLUSION OF A CRACKED, OLD MASK.

3. EYES:

TOOLS: BLACK EYESHADOWS, EYELINER, MASCARA.

INSTRUCTIONS: APPLY BLACK EYESHADOW ON THE EYELIDS, BLENDING IT UPWARDS TOWARDS THE BROWS TO CREATE A DEEP, MYSTERIOUS LOOK. USE EYELINER TO DRAW A DEFINED LINE ON THE UPPER AND LOWER LIDS, ACCENTUATING THE SHAPE OF THE EYES. FINISH WITH MASCARA TO ENHANCE THE LASHES AND ADD INTENSITY TO THE GAZE.

4. LIPS:

TOOLS: DARK BROWN OR BURGUNDY LIPSTICK.

INSTRUCTIONS: APPLY DARK BROWN OR BURGUNDY LIPSTICK, CAREFULLY OUTLINING THE LIPS. THE LIPS SHOULD HAVE A DARK, ANCIENT LOOK THAT COMPLEMENTS THE REST OF THE MAKEUP.

5. DETAILS:

TOOLS: BLACK FACE PAINT, FINE BRUSH.

INSTRUCTIONS: ADD SMALL CRACKS AND LINES ALONG THE EDGES OF THE MASK TO EMPHASIZE THE EFFECT OF AN ANCIENT, DAMAGED SURFACE. USE A FINE BRUSH FOR MAXIMUM PRECISION AND REALISM.

6. FINISHING TOUCHES:

TOOLS: HAIR STYLED IN WAVES, ACCESSORIES (E.G., ANCIENT-INSPIRED EARRINGS OR JEWELRY).

INSTRUCTIONS: COMPLETE THE LOOK BY STYLING THE HAIR IN SOFT WAVES, ENHANCING THE MYSTERIOUS, ANCIENT APPEARANCE. ADD ANCIENT-INSPIRED JEWELRY TO COMPLETE THE ENSEMBLE.

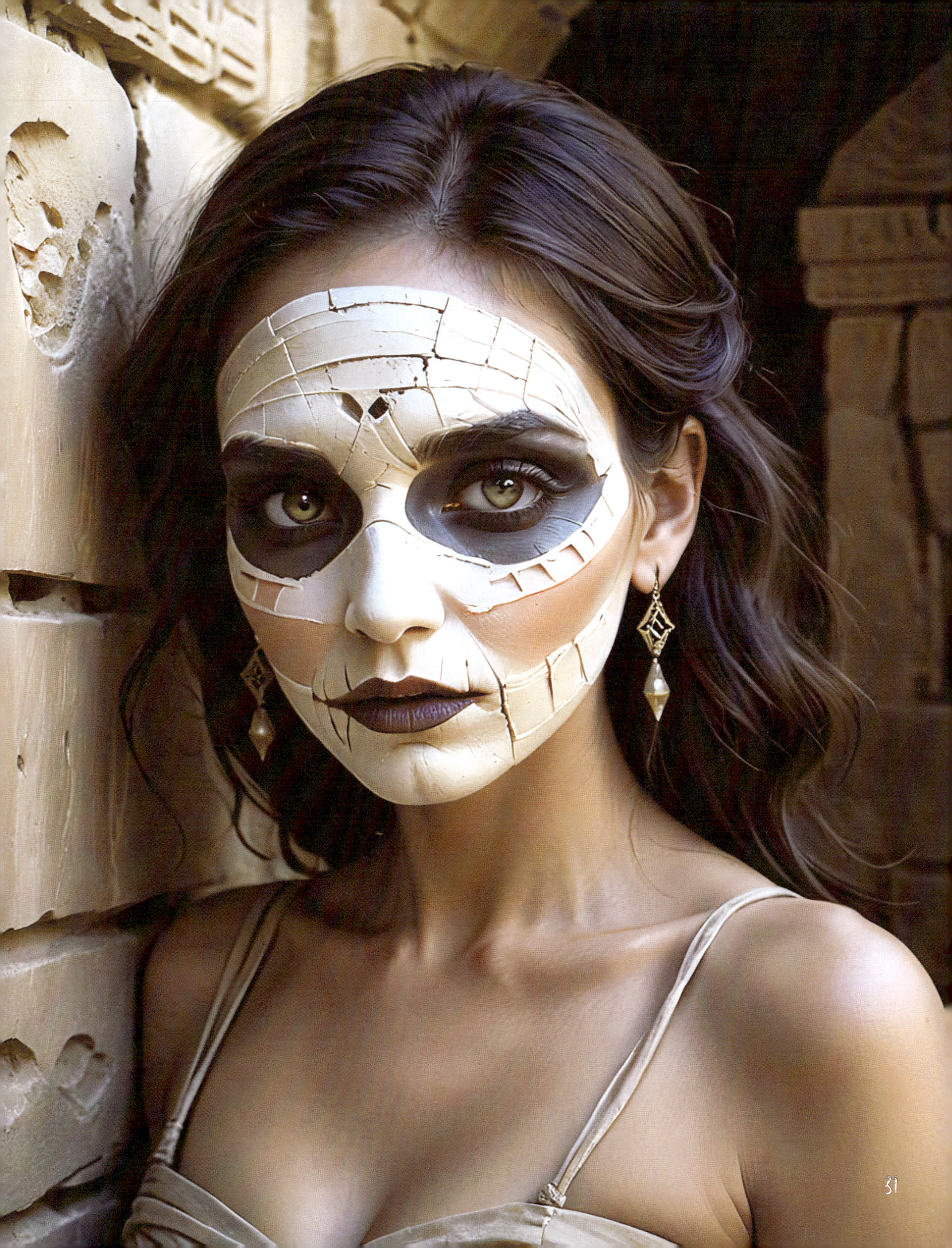

"DARK QUEEN OF THE NIGHT"

STEP-BY-STEP INSTRUCTIONS:

1. SKIN PREPARATION:

TOOLS: WHITE FACE PAINT, BRUSH OR SPONGE FOR APPLICATION.

INSTRUCTIONS: APPLY WHITE FACE PAINT ALL OVER THE FACE TO ACHIEVE A PALE, ALMOST SUPERNATURAL COMPLEXION. ENSURE THE PAINT IS EVENLY BLENDED, CREATING A SMOOTH BASE.

2. EYES:

TOOLS: BLACK EYESHADOW, EYELINER, MASCARA.

INSTRUCTIONS: APPLY BLACK EYESHADOW ON THE EYELIDS, BLENDING IT UPWARDS TOWARDS THE BROWS TO CREATE A DRAMATIC, DARK EFFECT. USE EYELINER TO DEFINE THE EYES, DRAWING A BOLD LINE ON THE UPPER AND LOWER LIDS. FINISH WITH MASCARA TO ENHANCE THE DEEP GAZE.

3. DARK FACIAL PATTERN:

TOOLS: BLACK FACE PAINT, FINE BRUSH.

INSTRUCTIONS: USE BLACK FACE PAINT TO CREATE AN ABSTRACT, DARK PATTERN ON ONE SIDE OF THE FACE, EXTENDING ACROSS THE FOREHEAD, EYE, AND CHEEK. THE PATTERN SHOULD BE DYNAMIC AND CONTRAST WITH THE PALE COMPLEXION, ADDING MYSTERY TO THE CHARACTER.

4. LIPS:

TOOLS: BLACK LIPSTICK.

INSTRUCTIONS: APPLY BLACK LIPSTICK, CAREFULLY OUTLINING THE LIPS. THE LIPS SHOULD BE PERFECTLY SHAPED TO EMPHASIZE THE DARK, GOTHIC CHARACTER OF THE MAKEUP.

5. DETAILS:

TOOLS: BLACK FACE PAINT, FINE BRUSH.

INSTRUCTIONS: ADD SMALL LINES AND DETAILS AROUND THE EYES AND LIPS THAT RESEMBLE CRACKS OR MYSTERIOUS PATTERNS, HIGHLIGHTING THE DARK NATURE OF THE CHARACTER.

6. FINISHING TOUCHES:

TOOLS: BLACK WIG OR NATURALLY DARK HAIR, ACCESSORIES (E.G., BLACK EARRINGS).

INSTRUCTIONS: COMPLETE THE LOOK BY WEARING A BLACK WIG OR STYLING NATURALLY DARK HAIR. ADD BLACK EARRINGS OR OTHER ACCESSORIES TO FINISH THE GOTHIC APPEARANCE.

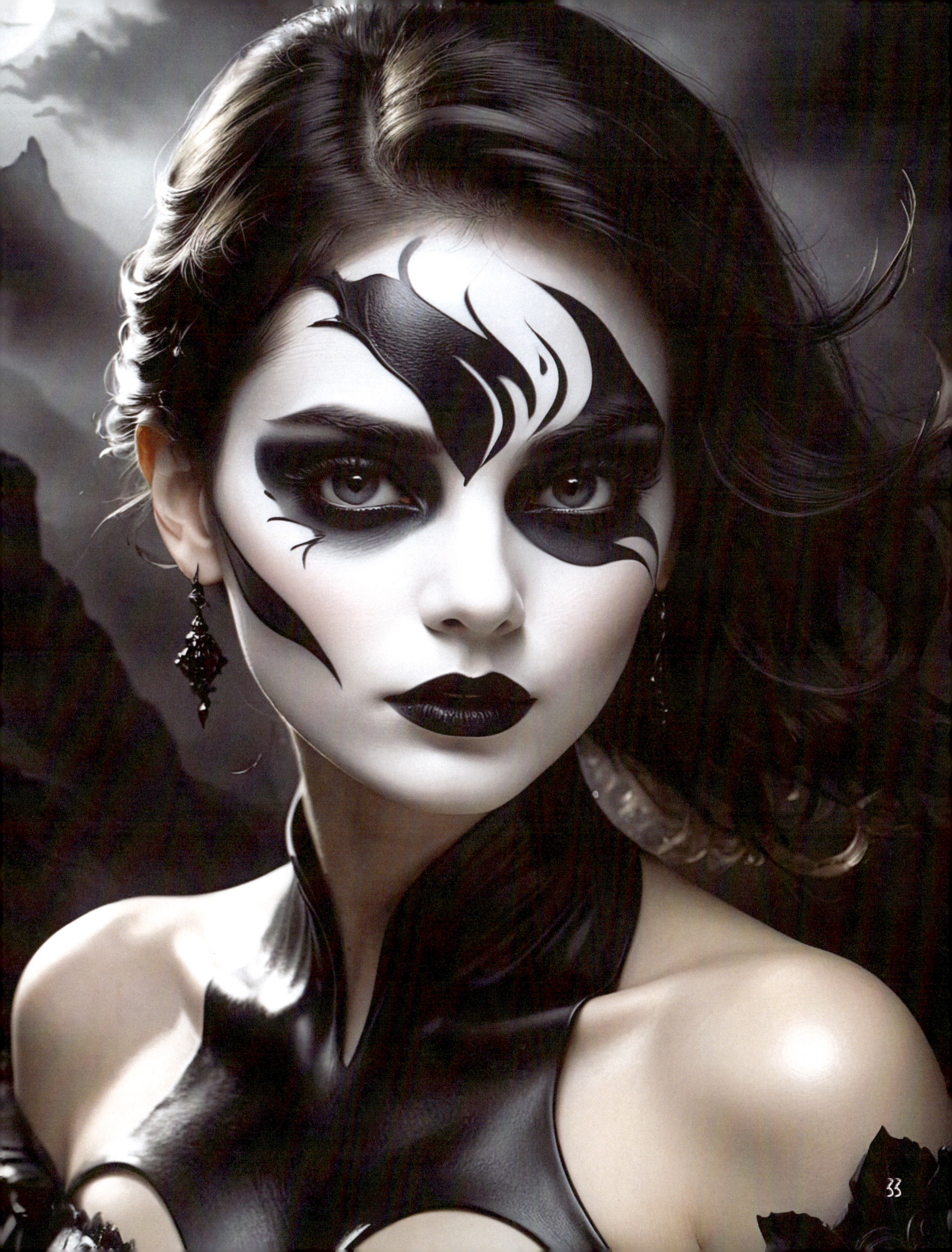
33

"GHOSTLY BRIDE"

STEP-BY-STEP INSTRUCTIONS:

1. SKIN PREPARATION:

TOOLS: WHITE FACE PAINT, BRUSH OR SPONGE FOR APPLICATION.

INSTRUCTIONS: APPLY WHITE FACE PAINT ALL OVER THE FACE TO ACHIEVE A PALE, GHOSTLY SKIN TONE. ENSURE THE PAINT IS EVENLY BLENDED, CREATING A SMOOTH AND MATTE BASE.

2. EYES:

TOOLS: BLUE AND GRAY EYESHADOWS, EYELINER, MASCARA.

INSTRUCTIONS: APPLY BLUE EYESHADOW ON THE EYELIDS, BLENDING IT GENTLY TOWARDS THE BROWS. ADD GRAY EYESHADOW ON THE LOWER EYELID TO HIGHLIGHT THE LOWER LASH LINE. USE EYELINER TO DRAW A SUBTLE LINE ON THE UPPER EYELID. FINISH WITH MASCARA TO ENHANCE THE LASHES AND ADD DEPTH TO THE EYES.

3. SPIDERWEB AND DETAILS:

TOOLS: WHITE FACE PAINT, FINE BRUSH.

INSTRUCTIONS: USE WHITE FACE PAINT TO DRAW A DELICATE SPIDERWEB PATTERN ON THE FOREHEAD, EXTENDING TOWARDS THE TEMPLES. ADD SMALL DROPLETS OF PAINT UNDER THE EYES TO SIMULATE TEARS, ENHANCING THE GHOSTLY EFFECT.

4. LIPS:

TOOLS: LIGHT PINK OR BEIGE LIPSTICK.

INSTRUCTIONS: APPLY LIGHT PINK OR BEIGE LIPSTICK, CAREFULLY OUTLINING THE LIPS. THE LIPS SHOULD BE SUBTLE TO KEEP THE FOCUS ON THE EYES AND SPIDERWEB.

5. FACIAL DETAILS:

TOOLS: GRAY EYESHADOW, FINE BRUSH.

INSTRUCTIONS: ADD SUBTLE SHADING ON THE CHEEKBONES AND AROUND THE JAWLINE TO EMPHASIZE THE HOLLOWS OF THE FACE, GIVING IT A MORE GHOSTLY, GAUNT APPEARANCE.

6. FINISHING TOUCHES:

TOOLS: VEIL, HAIR STYLED IN LOOSE WAVES, ACCESSORIES (E.G., VINTAGE-STYLE EARRINGS).

INSTRUCTIONS: COMPLETE THE LOOK WITH A VEIL THAT ADDS AN ELEMENT OF MYSTERY TO THE CHARACTER. STYLE THE HAIR IN LOOSE, SOFT WAVES TO ENHANCE THE GHOSTLY, ETHEREAL APPEARANCE. ADD VINTAGE-STYLE JEWELRY TO FINISH THE ENSEMBLE.

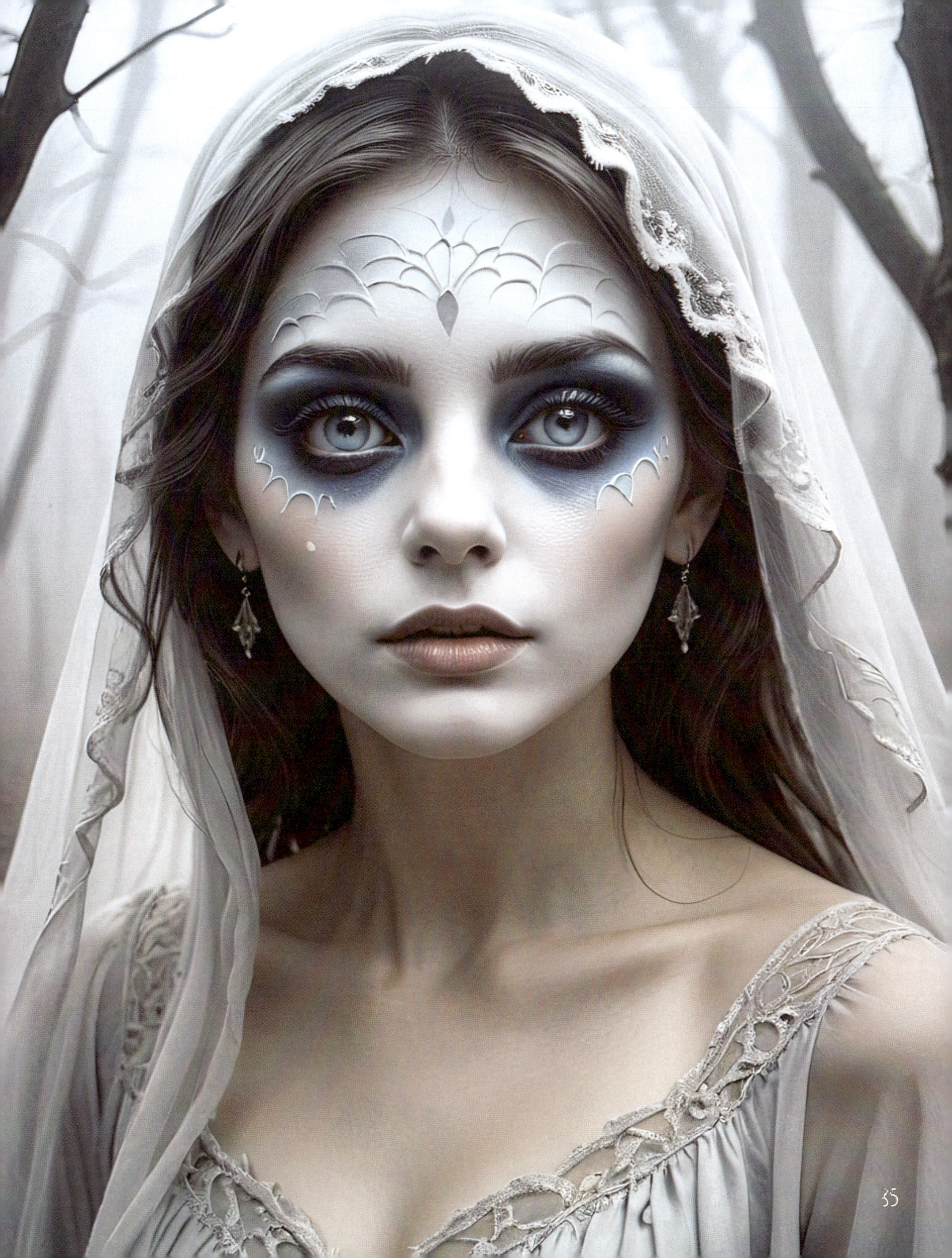

"DARK ANGEL"

STEP-BY-STEP INSTRUCTIONS:

1. SKIN PREPARATION:

TOOLS: WHITE FACE PAINT, BRUSH OR SPONGE FOR APPLICATION.

INSTRUCTIONS: APPLY WHITE FACE PAINT ALL OVER THE FACE TO ACHIEVE A SMOOTH, PALE COMPLEXION WITH A SUPERNATURAL APPEARANCE. ENSURE THE PAINT IS EVENLY BLENDED, CREATING A PERFECT BASE FOR THE REST OF THE MAKEUP.

2. EYES:

TOOLS: BLACK EYESHADOW, EYELINER, MASCARA.

INSTRUCTIONS: APPLY BLACK EYESHADOW ON THE EYELIDS, BLENDING IT UPWARDS TOWARDS THE BROWS TO CREATE A DRAMATIC, DARK EFFECT. USE EYELINER TO DRAW BOLD LINES ON THE UPPER AND LOWER LIDS. FINISH WITH MASCARA TO ENHANCE THE LASHES AND ADD INTENSITY TO THE GAZE.

3. FACIAL PATTERNS:

TOOLS: BLACK FACE PAINT, FINE BRUSH.

INSTRUCTIONS: USE BLACK FACE PAINT TO CREATE SYMMETRICAL, ORNAMENTAL PATTERNS AROUND THE EYES, ON THE FOREHEAD, AND ON THE CHEEKS. THE PATTERNS SHOULD BE INTRICATE AND DETAILED, RESEMBLING GOTHIC ORNAMENTS THAT ADD A MAJESTIC YET MENACING LOOK TO THE FACE.

4. LIPS:

TOOLS: BLACK LIPSTICK.

INSTRUCTIONS: APPLY BLACK LIPSTICK, CAREFULLY OUTLINING THE LIPS. THE DARK LIPS WILL COMPLETE THE GOTHIC, DARK CHARACTER OF THE MAKEUP.

5. DETAILS:

TOOLS: WHITE FACE PAINT, FINE BRUSH.

INSTRUCTIONS: ADD DELICATE WHITE ACCENTS AROUND THE BLACK PATTERNS TO EMPHASIZE CONTRAST AND GIVE THE FACE A THREE-DIMENSIONAL EFFECT. YOU CAN ALSO ADD A FEW SMALL DOTS AND LINES TO MAKE THE PATTERNS LOOK EVEN MORE INTRICATE AND MYSTERIOUS.

6. FINISHING TOUCHES:

TOOLS: WIG IN SILVER TONES OR NATURALLY GRAY HAIR, ANGEL WINGS, ACCESSORIES (E.G., EARRINGS).

INSTRUCTIONS: COMPLETE THE LOOK BY WEARING A WIG IN SILVER TONES OR STYLING THE HAIR IN NATURALLY GRAY HUES. ADD ANGEL WINGS AND ELEGANT EARRINGS TO FINISH THE MAJESTIC YET MENACING APPEARANCE.

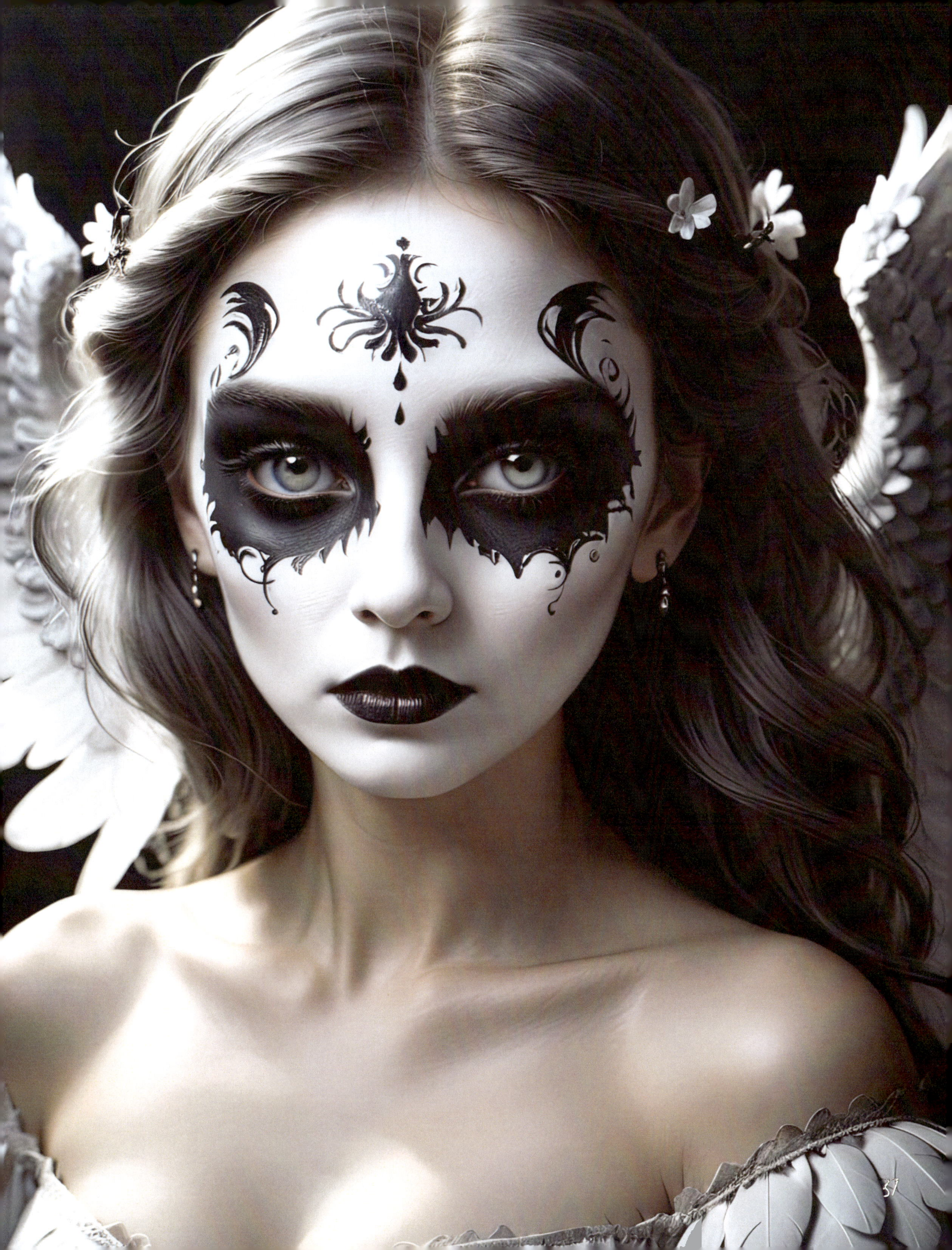

"NEON ALIEN"

STEP-BY-STEP INSTRUCTIONS:

1. SKIN PREPARATION:

TOOLS: BLUE FACE PAINT, BRUSH OR SPONGE FOR APPLICATION.

INSTRUCTIONS: APPLY BLUE FACE PAINT ALL OVER THE FACE TO ACHIEVE A UNIFORM, INTENSE, NEON COMPLEXION WITH A COSMIC APPEARANCE. ENSURE THE PAINT IS EVENLY BLENDED, CREATING A SMOOTH AND SHINY BASE.

2. EYES:

TOOLS: BLACK EYESHADOW, PINK EYELINER, MASCARA.

INSTRUCTIONS: APPLY BLACK EYESHADOW ON THE EYELIDS, BLENDING IT TOWARDS THE TEMPLES TO CREATE A DRAMATIC CONTRAST. USE PINK EYELINER TO OUTLINE THE UPPER AND LOWER LASH LINES, ADDING AN INTENSE, NEON ACCENT. FINISH WITH MASCARA TO ENHANCE THE EFFECT OF LARGE, EXPRESSIVE EYES.

3. NEON DETAILS:

TOOLS: PINK AND RED FACE PAINT, FINE BRUSH.

INSTRUCTIONS: USE PINK FACE PAINT TO CREATE NEON, DRIPPING PATTERNS AROUND THE EYES, ADDING INTENSITY AND MYSTERY TO THE LOOK. ADD RED FACE PAINT TO ACCENTUATE THESE PATTERNS, CREATING THE ILLUSION OF FLOWING ENERGY OR COSMIC SUBSTANCE.

4. EYEBROWS:

TOOLS: BLACK FACE PAINT OR EYELINER.

INSTRUCTIONS: DEFINE THE EYEBROWS, GIVING THEM A SHARP, CURVED SHAPE THAT ENHANCES THE COSMIC, FUTURISTIC APPEARANCE. THE EYEBROWS SHOULD BE BOLD AND PROVIDE CONTRAST TO THE NEON DETAILS.

5. LIPS:

TOOLS: PINK LIPSTICK, LIP GLOSS.

INSTRUCTIONS: APPLY PINK LIPSTICK TO THE LIPS, CAREFULLY OUTLINING THEIR SHAPE. ADD GLOSS TO GIVE THE LIPS A SHINY, NEON GLOW THAT COMPLEMENTS THE OVERALL MAKEUP.

6. FINISHING TOUCHES:

TOOLS: PINK WIG OR NEON PINK HAIR DYE, NEON ACCESSORIES (E.G., EARRINGS, NECKLACE).

INSTRUCTIONS: COMPLETE THE LOOK BY WEARING A NEON PINK WIG OR DYEING THE HAIR A VIBRANT, NEON PINK. ADD NEON-STYLE ACCESSORIES, SUCH AS EARRINGS OR A NECKLACE, TO EMPHASIZE THE FUTURISTIC, COSMIC APPEARANCE

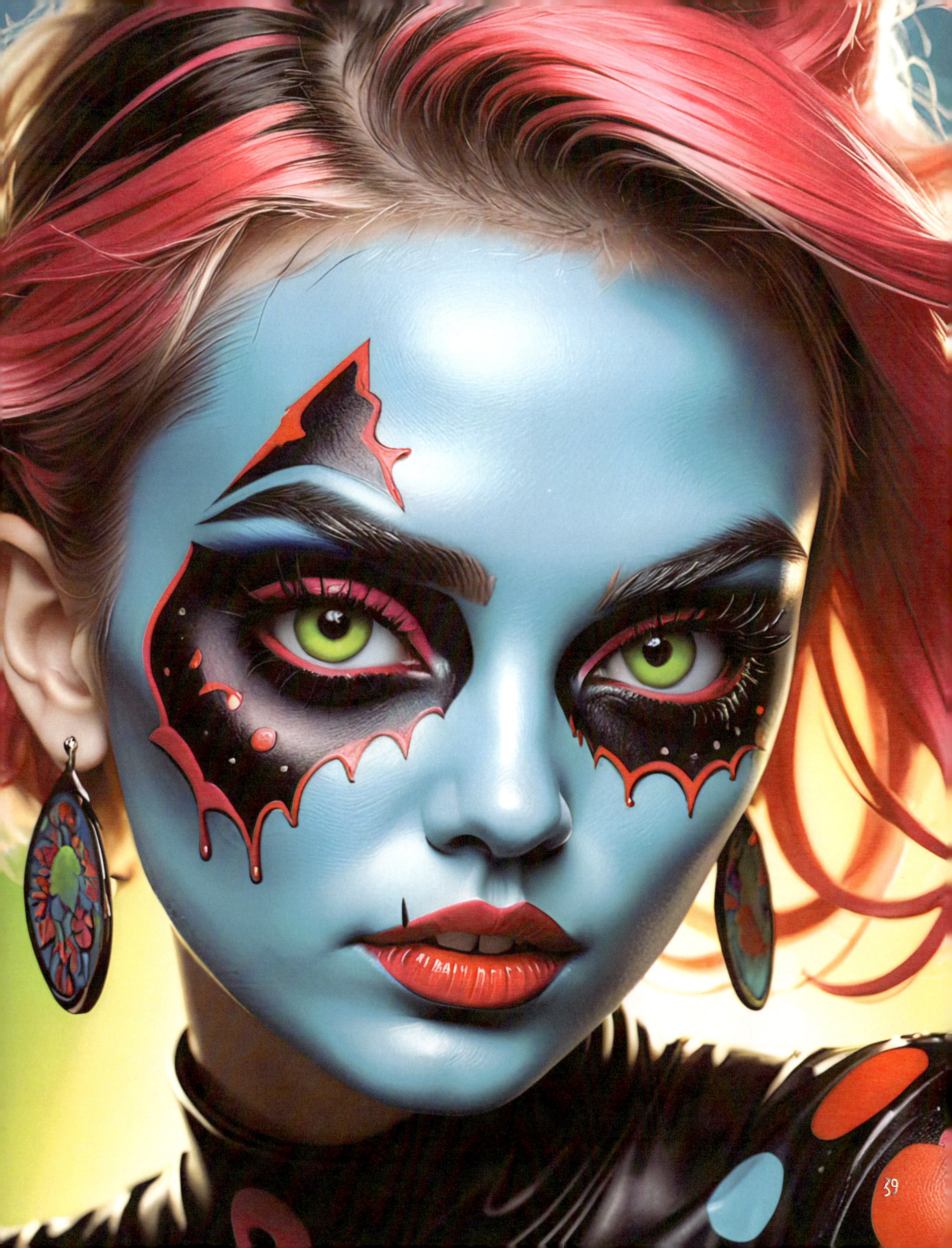

"BLOODY RED RIDING HOOD"

STEP-BY-STEP INSTRUCTIONS:

1. SKIN PREPARATION:

TOOLS: LIGHT FOUNDATION, TRANSLUCENT POWDER.

INSTRUCTIONS: APPLY LIGHT FOUNDATION ALL OVER THE FACE TO ACHIEVE A PORCELAIN, SMOOTH COMPLEXION. ENSURE THE FOUNDATION IS EVENLY BLENDED, THEN SET IT WITH TRANSLUCENT POWDER TO GIVE THE SKIN A MATTE FINISH.

2. EYES:

TOOLS: RED AND BLACK EYESHADOWS, RED EYELINER, MASCARA.

INSTRUCTIONS: APPLY RED EYESHADOW ON THE ENTIRE EYELID, BLENDING IT GENTLY TOWARDS THE BROWS. USE BLACK EYESHADOW TO ACCENTUATE THE OUTER CORNERS OF THE EYES AND ADD DEPTH. USE RED EYELINER TO OUTLINE THE LOWER LASH LINE, CREATING A DRAMATIC EFFECT. FINISH WITH MASCARA TO ENHANCE THE LASHES AND ADD INTENSITY TO THE GAZE.

3. BLOODY TEARS:

TOOLS: RED FACE PAINT OR EYELINER, FINE BRUSH.

INSTRUCTIONS: USE RED FACE PAINT OR EYELINER TO DRAW DELICATE, DRIPPING LINES FROM THE LOWER EYELID, RESEMBLING BLOODY TEARS. THE LINES SHOULD BE THIN AND PRECISE TO ADD DRAMA AND MYSTERY.

4. EYEBROWS:

TOOLS: BLACK FACE PAINT OR EYELINER.

INSTRUCTIONS: DEFINE THE EYEBROWS, GIVING THEM A BOLD, SHARP SHAPE THAT ENHANCES THE INTENSE LOOK OF THE EYES. THE EYEBROWS SHOULD BE CLEARLY OUTLINED TO CONTRAST WITH THE LIGHT COMPLEXION.

5. LIPS:

TOOLS: RED LIPSTICK.

INSTRUCTIONS: APPLY DEEP RED LIPSTICK, CAREFULLY OUTLINING THE LIPS. THE LIP COLOR SHOULD MATCH THE BLOODY TEARS, CREATING A COHESIVE AND DRAMATIC EFFECT.

6. FINISHING TOUCHES:

TOOLS: RED HOOD, ACCESSORIES (E.G., GOTHIC-STYLE EARRINGS).

INSTRUCTIONS: COMPLETE THE LOOK WITH A RED HOOD, ADDING AN ELEMENT OF MYSTERY AND REFERENCING THE RED RIDING HOOD MOTIF. ADD GOTHIC EARRINGS OR OTHER ACCESSORIES TO FINISH THE DARK, FAIRY-TALE APPEARANCE.

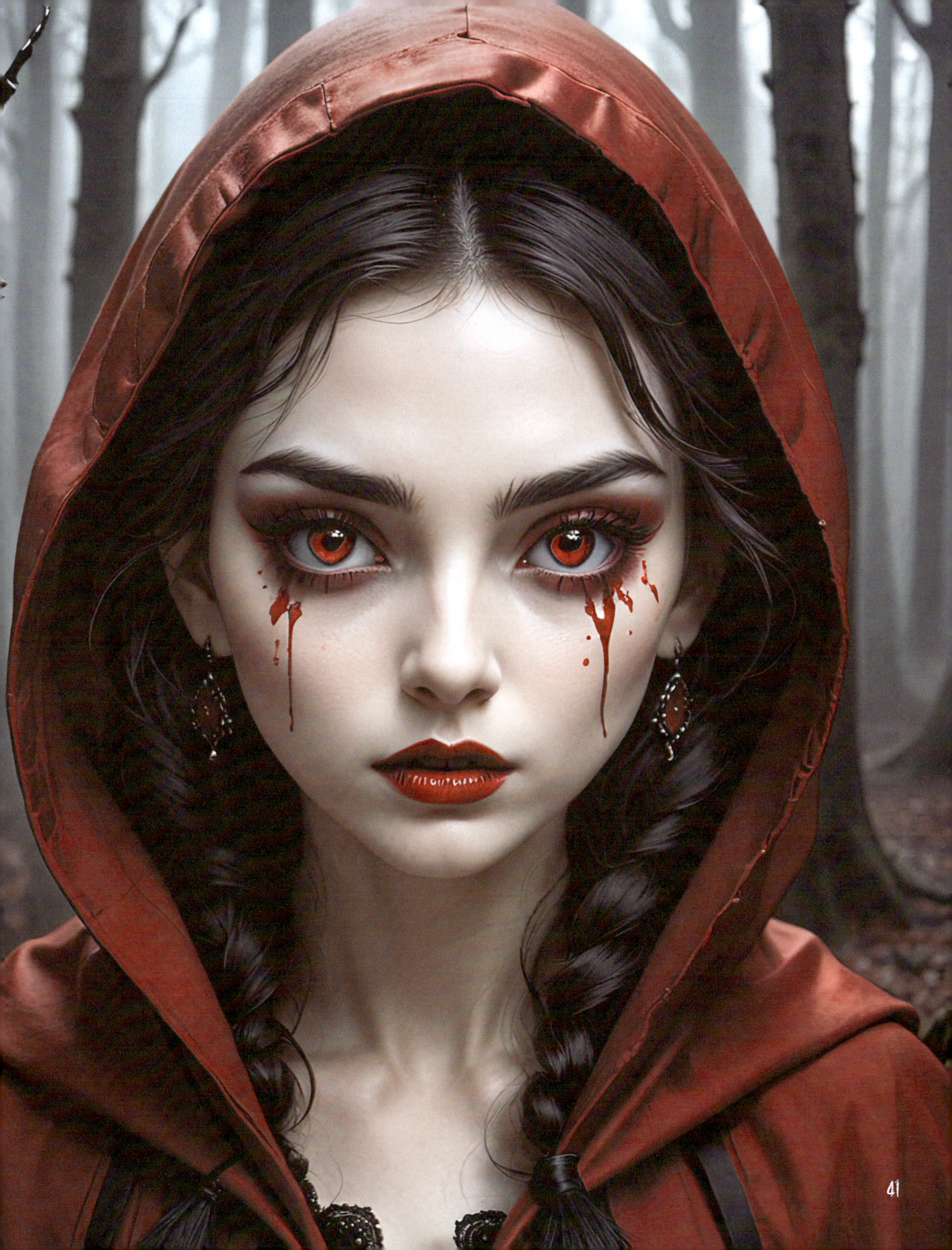

"BLOODY TEARS"

STEP-BY-STEP INSTRUCTIONS:

1. SKIN PREPARATION:

TOOLS: LIGHT FOUNDATION, TRANSLUCENT POWDER.

INSTRUCTIONS: APPLY LIGHT FOUNDATION ALL OVER THE FACE TO ACHIEVE A PORCELAIN, SMOOTH COMPLEXION. ENSURE THE FOUNDATION IS EVENLY BLENDED, THEN SET IT WITH TRANSLUCENT POWDER TO GIVE THE SKIN A MATTE FINISH.

2. EYES:

TOOLS: RED EYESHADOWS, BLACK EYELINER, MASCARA.

INSTRUCTIONS: APPLY INTENSE RED EYESHADOW ON THE ENTIRE EYELID, BLENDING IT GENTLY AROUND THE EYES, INCLUDING THE LOWER LID, TO CREATE A DEEP, DRAMATIC EFFECT. USE BLACK EYELINER TO LIGHTLY DEFINE THE LASH LINE, THEN APPLY MASCARA TO ADD VOLUME AND LENGTH TO THE LASHES.

3. BLOODY TEARS:

TOOLS: RED FACE PAINT OR LIQUID RED EYELINER, FINE BRUSH.

INSTRUCTIONS: USE RED FACE PAINT OR LIQUID EYELINER TO CREATE DRIPPING, BLOODY TEARS STARTING FROM THE LOWER EYELIDS. THE LINE SHOULD BE IRREGULAR TO MIMIC THE NATURAL FLOW OF BLOOD, ADDING DRAMA AND INTENSITY TO THE OVERALL LOOK.

4. EYEBROWS:

TOOLS: BLACK FACE PAINT OR EYELINER.

INSTRUCTIONS: DEFINE THE EYEBROWS, GIVING THEM A BOLD, SHARP SHAPE THAT CONTRASTS WITH THE RED EYESHADOW AND BLOODY TEARS. THE EYEBROWS SHOULD BE WELL-DEFINED TO ADD EXPRESSIVENESS TO THE FACE.

5. LIPS:

TOOLS: RED LIPSTICK, LIP GLOSS.

INSTRUCTIONS: APPLY DEEP RED LIPSTICK, CAREFULLY OUTLINING THE LIPS. ADD GLOSS TO THE CENTER OF THE LIPS FOR A SHINY EFFECT, ENHANCING THE DRAMATIC NATURE OF THE MAKEUP.

6. FINISHING TOUCHES:

TOOLS: HAIR STYLED SLEEK WITH A SLIGHT SHINE, MEDICAL-STYLE OUTFIT (E.G., WHITE LAB COAT), ACCESSORIES (E.G., DARK EARRINGS).

INSTRUCTIONS: COMPLETE THE LOOK BY STYLING THE HAIR SLEEK WITH A SLIGHT SHINE TO EMPHASIZE THE STERNNESS AND DRAMA OF THE CHARACTER. ADD A MEDICAL-STYLE OUTFIT, SUCH AS A WHITE LAB COAT, TO COMPLETE THE DARK, INTRIGUING APPEARANCE. EARRINGS OR OTHER SUBTLE ACCESSORIES CAN ADD ELEGANCE, CONTRASTING WITH THE INTENSE MAKEUP

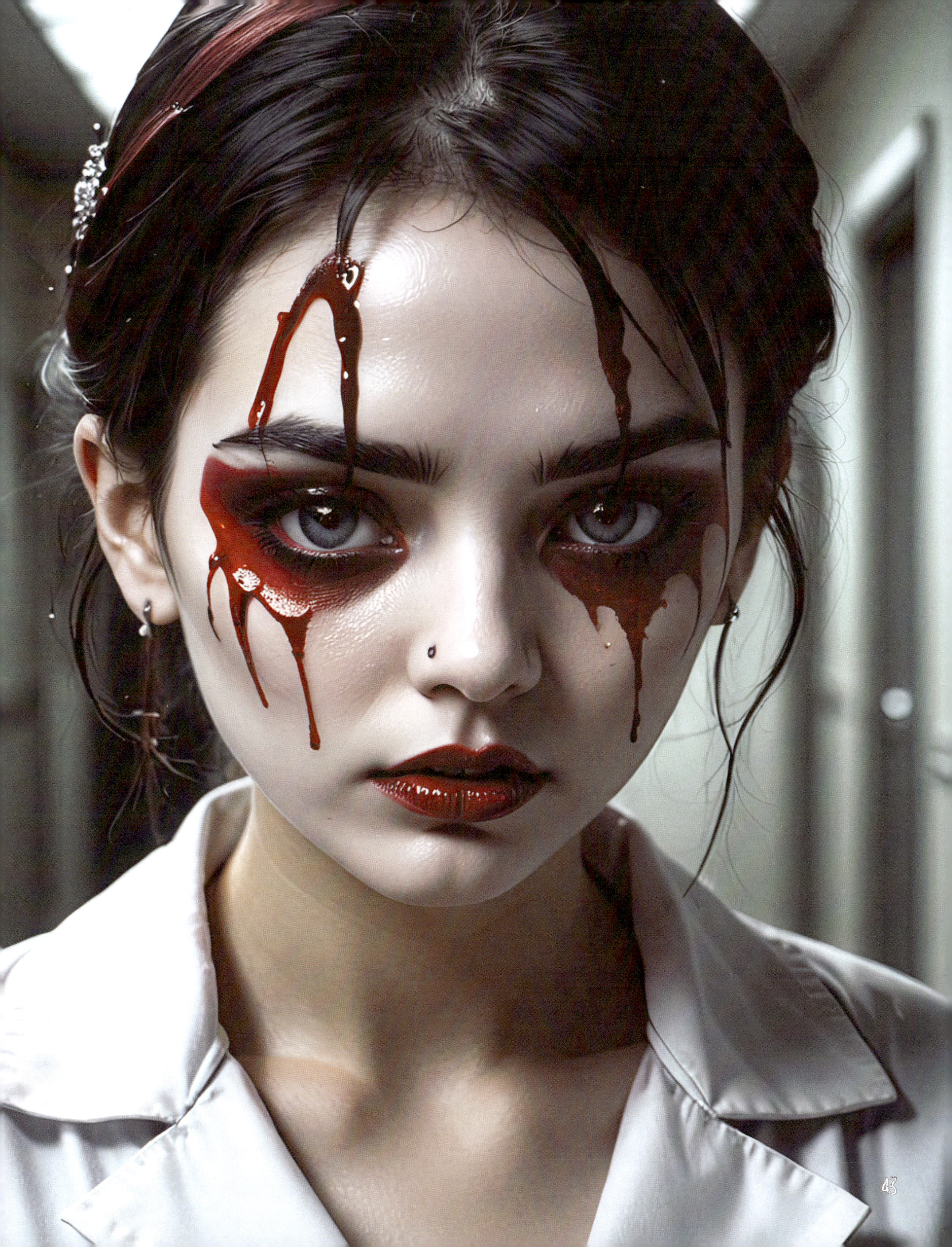

"GOTHIC PORCELAIN DOLL"

STEP-BY-STEP INSTRUCTIONS:

1. SKIN PREPARATION:

TOOLS: WHITE FACE PAINT, BRUSH OR SPONGE FOR APPLICATION.

INSTRUCTIONS: APPLY WHITE FACE PAINT ALL OVER THE FACE TO ACHIEVE A SMOOTH, PORCELAIN-LIKE COMPLEXION. ENSURE THE PAINT IS EVENLY BLENDED, CREATING A PERFECTLY MATTE BASE THAT GIVES THE FACE A DOLL-LIKE APPEARANCE.

2. EYES:

TOOLS: BLACK EYESHADOW, EYELINER, RED CONTACT LENSES, MASCARA.

INSTRUCTIONS: APPLY BLACK EYESHADOW ON THE EYELIDS, BLENDING IT TOWARDS THE BROWS TO CREATE A DEEP, GOTHIC EFFECT. USE EYELINER TO DRAW BOLD LINES ON THE UPPER AND LOWER LIDS, ALSO ADDING LONG, SHARP LINES TO MIMIC EXTENDED LASHES ON THE LOWER LID. FINISH WITH MASCARA TO ACCENTUATE THE LASHES. WEAR RED CONTACT LENSES TO GIVE THE EYES A HAUNTING, DOLL-LIKE LOOK.

3. EYEBROWS:

TOOLS: BLACK FACE PAINT OR EYELINER.

INSTRUCTIONS: DEFINE THE EYEBROWS, GIVING THEM A BOLD, SHARP SHAPE. THE EYEBROWS SHOULD BE WELL-DEFINED AND CONTRAST WITH THE PALE COMPLEXION, ENHANCING THE INTENSE CHARACTER OF THE MAKEUP.

4. LIPS:

TOOLS: RED LIPSTICK, BLACK FACE PAINT.

INSTRUCTIONS: APPLY DEEP RED LIPSTICK, CAREFULLY OUTLINING THE LIPS. USE BLACK FACE PAINT TO OUTLINE THE EDGES OF THE LIPS, GIVING THEM A DRAMATIC AND GOTHIC APPEARANCE.

5. CHEEKS:

TOOLS: COOL-TONED BLUSH.

INSTRUCTIONS: LIGHTLY APPLY BLUSH TO THE CHEEKS, FOCUSING ON THE APPLES TO GIVE THE FACE A SUBTLE, DOLL-LIKE FLUSH THAT ACCENTUATES THE PORCELAIN LOOK.

6. FINISHING TOUCHES:

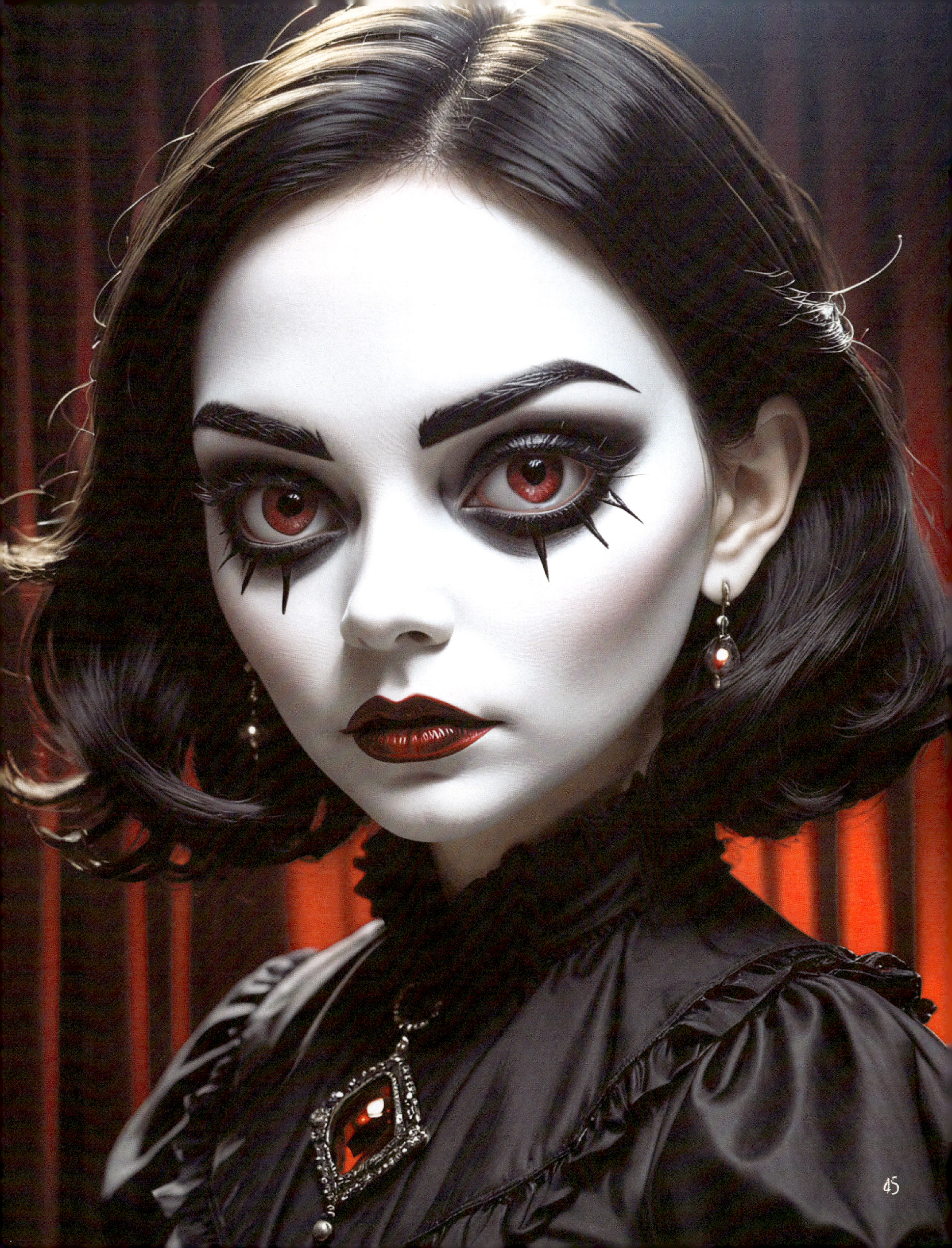
45

"DEMONIC QUEEN"

STEP-BY-STEP INSTRUCTIONS:

1. SKIN PREPARATION:

TOOLS: WHITE FACE PAINT, BRUSH OR SPONGE FOR APPLICATION.

INSTRUCTIONS: APPLY WHITE FACE PAINT ALL OVER THE FACE TO ACHIEVE A SMOOTH, PALE COMPLEXION WITH A SUPERNATURAL APPEARANCE. ENSURE THE PAINT IS EVENLY BLENDED, CREATING A PERFECT BASE FOR THE REST OF THE MAKEUP.

2. EYES:

TOOLS: RED AND BLACK EYESHADOWS, EYELINER, RED CONTACT LENSES, MASCARA.

INSTRUCTIONS: APPLY RED EYESHADOW ON THE EYELIDS, BLENDING IT OUTWARDS TOWARDS THE CORNERS OF THE EYES. USE BLACK EYESHADOW TO DEEPEN THE GAZE, APPLYING IT TO THE OUTER CORNERS AND BLENDING IT WITH THE RED SHADOW. USE EYELINER TO DRAW A BOLD LINE ON THE UPPER AND LOWER LIDS, ACCENTUATING THE DRAMA OF THE LOOK. WEAR RED CONTACT LENSES TO ACHIEVE A DEMONIC APPEARANCE. FINISH WITH MASCARA TO ENHANCE THE EFFECT.

3. DEMONIC FACIAL PATTERNS:

TOOLS: BLACK AND RED FACE PAINT, FINE BRUSH.

INSTRUCTIONS: USE BLACK AND RED FACE PAINT TO CREATE SYMMETRICAL, SHARP PATTERNS ON THE FOREHEAD, CHEEKS, AND AROUND THE EYES. THE PATTERNS SHOULD BE AGGRESSIVE AND INTRICATE, EMPHASIZING THE DEMONIC NATURE OF THE CHARACTER.

4. LIPS:

TOOLS: RED LIPSTICK, BLACK FACE PAINT.

INSTRUCTIONS: APPLY RED LIPSTICK, CAREFULLY OUTLINING THE LIPS. USE BLACK FACE PAINT TO ADD THIN LINES ON THE LOWER LIP, GIVING THE LIPS A DEMONIC AND UNSETTLING LOOK.

5. EYEBROWS:

TOOLS: BLACK FACE PAINT OR EYELINER.

INSTRUCTIONS: DEFINE THE EYEBROWS, GIVING THEM A BOLD, ARCHED SHAPE THAT ADDS AN INTENSE, MENACING EXPRESSION TO THE FACE. THE EYEBROWS SHOULD BE WELL-DEFINED AND STRIKING.

6. FINISHING TOUCHES:

TOOLS: HORNS (FAKE OR LATEX-FORMED), BLACK HAIR OR WIG, ACCESSORIES (E.G., PENTAGRAM EARRINGS, AMULET).

INSTRUCTIONS: COMPLETE THE LOOK BY WEARING FAKE HORNS AND BLACK HAIR OR A WIG TO FINALIZE THE DEMONIC APPEARANCE. ADD ACCESSORIES SUCH AS PENTAGRAM EARRINGS OR AN AMULET TO ENHANCE THE DARK CHARACTER.

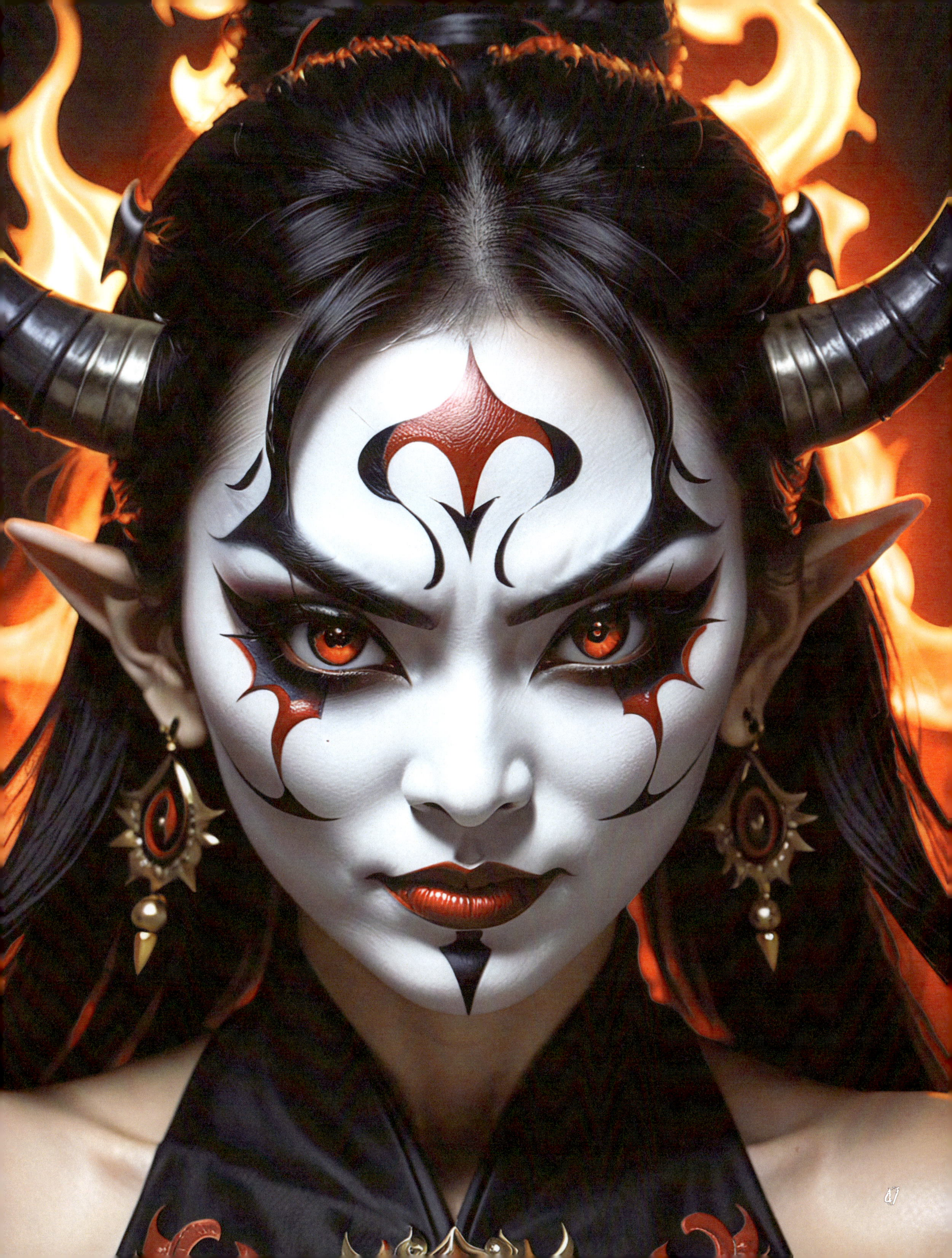

"WINTER FROST QUEEN"

STEP-BY-STEP INSTRUCTIONS:

1. SKIN PREPARATION:

TOOLS: WHITE FACE PAINT, BRUSH OR SPONGE FOR APPLICATION.

INSTRUCTIONS: APPLY WHITE FACE PAINT ALL OVER THE FACE TO ACHIEVE A PALE, WINTER COMPLEXION. ENSURE THE PAINT IS EVENLY BLENDED, CREATING A SMOOTH AND MATTE BASE THAT GIVES THE FACE AN ICY APPEARANCE.

2. EYES:

TOOLS: BLACK AND GRAY EYESHADOWS, EYELINER, WHITE CONTACT LENSES, MASCARA.

INSTRUCTIONS: APPLY BLACK EYESHADOW ON THE EYELIDS, BLENDING IT TOWARDS THE BROWS AND TEMPLES TO CREATE A DEEP, DARK EFFECT. USE GRAY EYESHADOW TO ACCENTUATE THE LOWER LID AND ADD A COLD LOOK TO THE EYES. USE EYELINER TO DRAW A THIN LINE ON THE UPPER LID. WEAR WHITE CONTACT LENSES TO GIVE THE EYES A COLD, ICY EXPRESSION. FINISH WITH MASCARA TO ENHANCE THE FROSTY GAZE.

3. ICY FACIAL PATTERNS:

TOOLS: GRAY FACE PAINT, FINE BRUSH.

INSTRUCTIONS: USE GRAY FACE PAINT TO CREATE SUBTLE, CRACKING PATTERNS ON THE FOREHEAD, AROUND THE EYES, AND ON THE CHEEKS, MIMICKING CRACKING ICE. THE PATTERNS SHOULD BE DELICATE AND RESEMBLE FROZEN BRANCHES OR ICE, EMPHASIZING THE WINTERY CHARACTER OF THE FIGURE.

4. LIPS:

TOOLS: DARK GRAY OR BLACK LIPSTICK.

INSTRUCTIONS: APPLY DARK GRAY OR BLACK LIPSTICK, CAREFULLY OUTLINING THE LIPS. THE DARK LIPS WILL COMPLETE THE ICY, FROSTY CHARACTER OF THE MAKEUP.

5. NECK AND DéCOLLETAGE:

TOOLS: GRAY AND BLUE EYESHADOWS, BLENDING BRUSH.

INSTRUCTIONS: APPLY GRAY AND BLUE SHADOWS ON THE NECK AND DéCOLLETAGE, CREATING A SHADING EFFECT THAT CONTINUES THE MAKEUP FROM THE FACE. BLEND THE COLORS TO ACHIEVE SOFT TRANSITIONS, RESEMBLING THE ICY BREATH OF WINTER.

6. FINISHING TOUCHES:

TOOLS: SILVER WIG OR NATURALLY GRAY HAIR, ACCESSORIES (E.G., NECKLACE WITH DARK GEMSTONE, EARRINGS).

INSTRUCTIONS: COMPLETE THE LOOK BY WEARING A SILVER WIG OR STYLING THE HAIR IN GRAY. ADD ACCESSORIES LIKE A NECKLACE WITH A DARK GEMSTONE OR DELICATE EARRINGS TO FINISH THE ICY, ROYAL APPEARANCE.

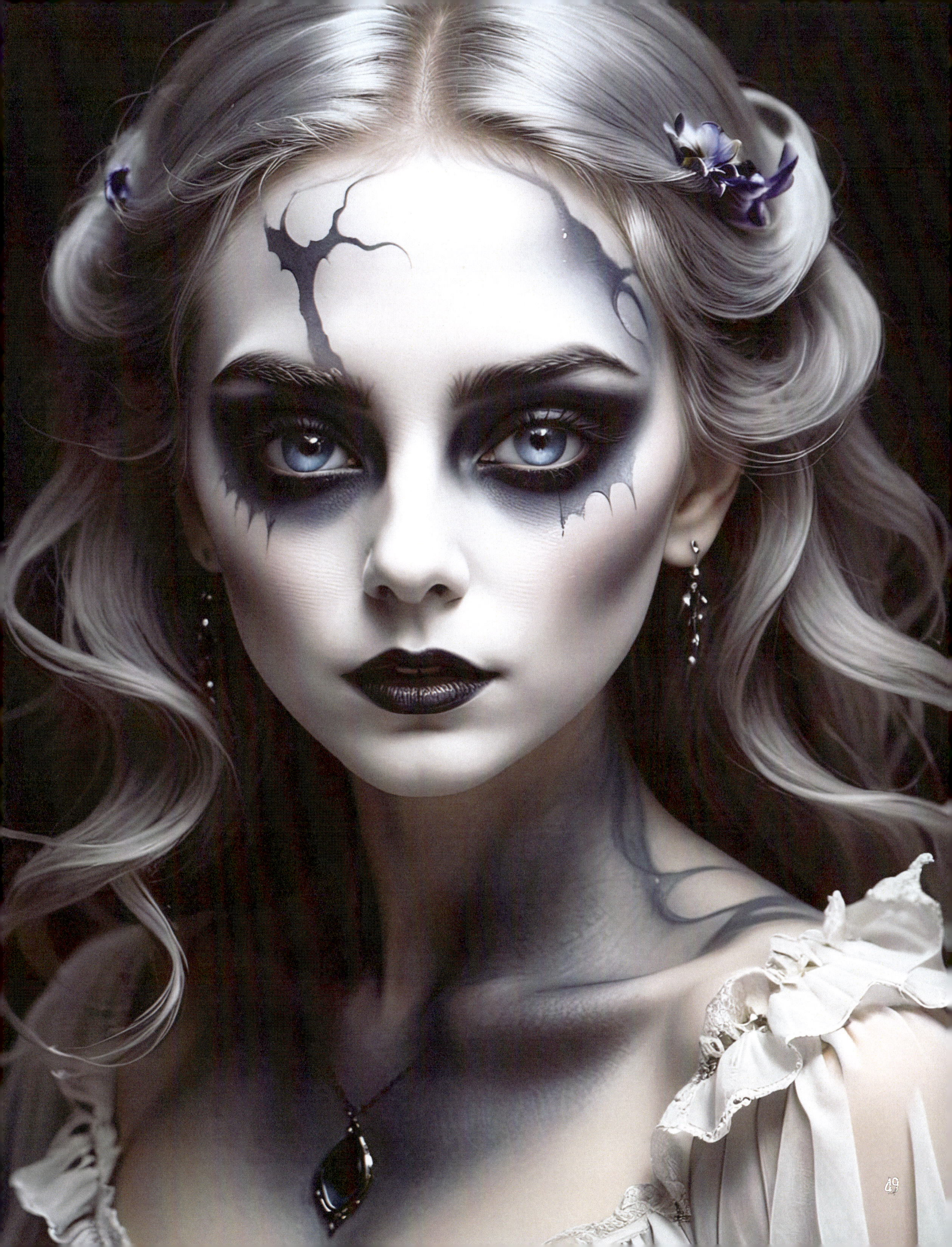

„NIGHT BUTTERFLY"

STEP-BY-STEP INSTRUCTIONS:

1. SKIN PREPARATION:

TOOLS: LIGHT FOUNDATION, TRANSLUCENT POWDER.

INSTRUCTIONS: APPLY LIGHT FOUNDATION ALL OVER THE FACE TO ACHIEVE A SMOOTH, EVEN COMPLEXION. ENSURE THE FOUNDATION IS EVENLY BLENDED, CREATING A PERFECT BASE FOR THE REST OF THE MAKEUP.

2. EYES:

TOOLS: PURPLE EYESHADOW, EYELINER, MASCARA.

INSTRUCTIONS: APPLY INTENSE PURPLE EYESHADOW ON THE EYELIDS, BLENDING IT TOWARDS THE TEMPLES. USE EYELINER TO DRAW A PRECISE LINE ON THE UPPER EYELID, THEN APPLY MASCARA TO ENHANCE THE LASHES. ADD FAKE BUTTERFLIES AS DECORATIONS AROUND THE EYES TO EMPHASIZE THE BUTTERFLY THEME.

3. EYEBROWS:

TOOLS: BLACK FACE PAINT OR EYELINER.

INSTRUCTIONS: DEFINE THE EYEBROWS, GIVING THEM A BOLD SHAPE THAT CONTRASTS WITH THE SOFT COLOR OF THE EYESHADOW.

4. LIPS:

TOOLS: PURPLE LIPSTICK.

INSTRUCTIONS: APPLY PURPLE LIPSTICK, CAREFULLY OUTLINING THE LIPS. THE INTENSE LIP COLOR SHOULD COMPLEMENT THE EYESHADOW, CREATING A COHESIVE EFFECT.

5. DETAILS:

TOOLS: FAKE BUTTERFLIES, COSMETIC GLUE.

INSTRUCTIONS: ATTACH FAKE BUTTERFLIES TO THE FACE AND HAIR USING COSMETIC GLUE TO CREATE THE ILLUSION OF BUTTERFLIES RESTING ON YOUR SKIN.

6. FINISHING TOUCHES:

TOOLS: WAVY HAIR, ACCESSORIES (E.G., BUTTERFLY HAIRPINS).

INSTRUCTIONS: COMPLETE THE LOOK BY STYLING THE HAIR IN WAVES AND ADDING BUTTERFLY-THEMED ACCESSORIES THAT ENHANCE THE NIGHT, MAGICAL APPEARANCE.

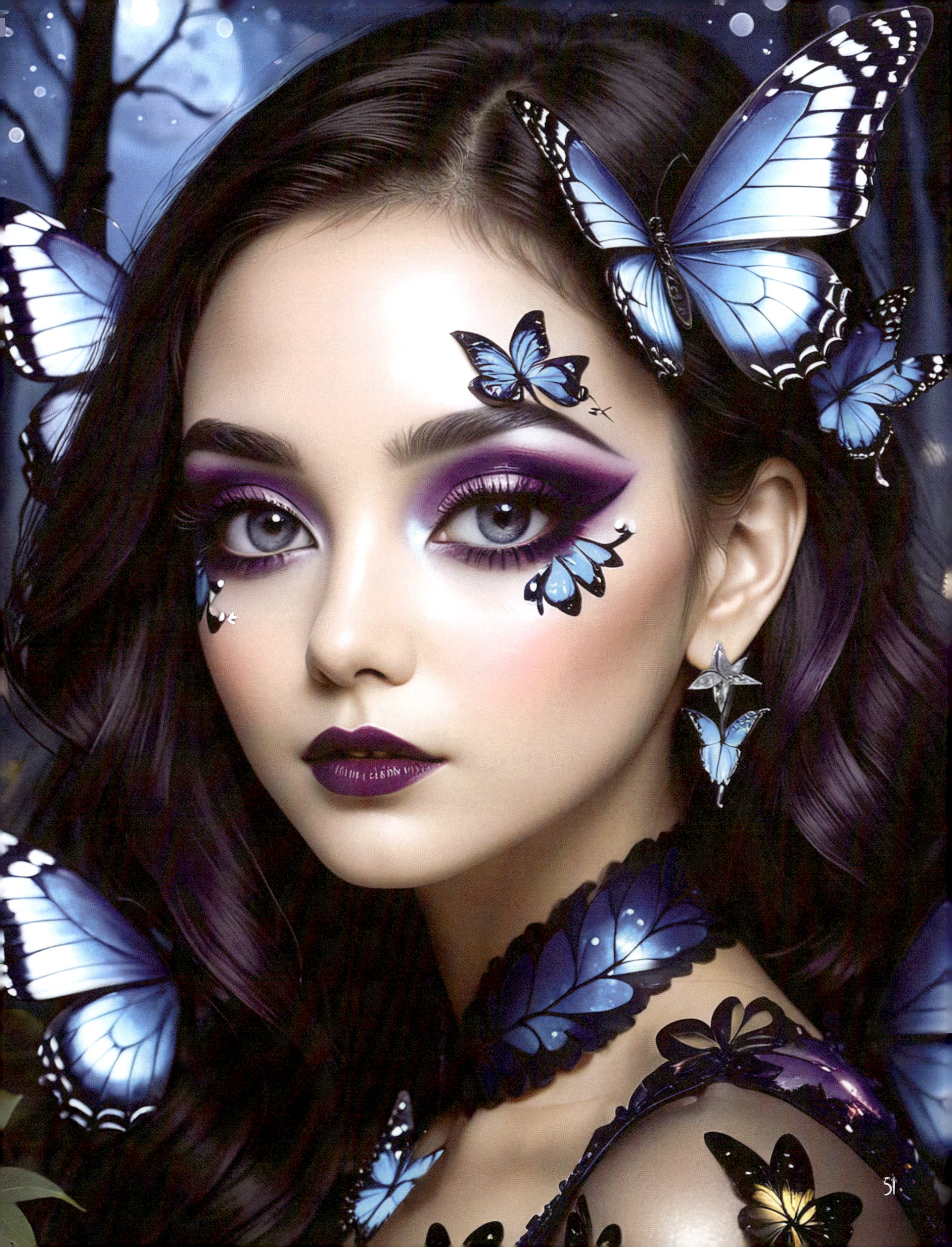

"DARK FOREST WITCH"

STEP-BY-STEP INSTRUCTIONS:

1. SKIN PREPARATION:

TOOLS: LIGHT FOUNDATION, TRANSLUCENT POWDER.

INSTRUCTIONS: APPLY LIGHT FOUNDATION ALL OVER THE FACE TO ACHIEVE A SMOOTH, PORCELAIN-LIKE COMPLEXION. ENSURE THE FOUNDATION IS EVENLY BLENDED, THEN SET IT WITH TRANSLUCENT POWDER TO GIVE THE SKIN A MATTE FINISH.

2. EYES:

TOOLS: PURPLE EYESHADOW, BLACK EYELINER, MASCARA, GREEN CONTACT LENSES.

INSTRUCTIONS: APPLY PURPLE EYESHADOW ON THE EYELIDS, BLENDING IT TOWARDS THE TEMPLES TO CREATE A DEEP, MYSTERIOUS EFFECT. USE BLACK EYELINER TO DRAW A BOLD LINE ON THE UPPER LID, AND ADD SEVERAL LONG LINES EXTENDING FROM THE LOWER LID TO MIMIC DARK LASHES. APPLY MASCARA TO ENHANCE THE LASHES, THEN WEAR GREEN CONTACT LENSES TO GIVE THE GAZE A MAGICAL, WITCH-LIKE APPEARANCE.

3. EYEBROWS:

TOOLS: BLACK FACE PAINT OR EYELINER.

INSTRUCTIONS: DEFINE THE EYEBROWS, GIVING THEM A BOLD, SHARP SHAPE. THE EYEBROWS SHOULD BE WELL-DEFINED TO CONTRAST WITH THE PURPLE EYESHADOW AND INTENSE GAZE.

4. LIPS:

TOOLS: DARK PURPLE LIPSTICK.

INSTRUCTIONS: APPLY DARK PURPLE LIPSTICK, CAREFULLY OUTLINING THE LIPS. THE LIP COLOR SHOULD BE DEEP AND MYSTERIOUS, MATCHING THE REST OF THE MAKEUP.

5. MAGICAL DETAILS:

TOOLS: BLACK FACE PAINT, FINE BRUSH.

INSTRUCTIONS: USE BLACK FACE PAINT TO DRAW A DELICATE, MYSTICAL PATTERN ON THE FOREHEAD, JUST ABOVE THE BROWS. THE PATTERN SHOULD RESEMBLE A MAGICAL SYMBOL OR STAR, EMPHASIZING THE WITCHY CHARACTER OF THE FIGURE.

6. FINISHING TOUCHES:

TOOLS: BLACK-PURPLE WIG OR DARK HAIR WITH PURPLE HIGHLIGHTS, WITCH'S HAT, ACCESSORIES (E.G., GREEN DANGLING EARRINGS, NECKLACE WITH A MAGICAL STONE).

INSTRUCTIONS: COMPLETE THE LOOK BY WEARING A BLACK-PURPLE WIG OR STYLING THE HAIR DARK WITH PURPLE HIGHLIGHTS. ADD A CLASSIC WITCH'S HAT AND ACCESSORIES LIKE GREEN DANGLING EARRINGS AND A NECKLACE WITH A MAGICAL STONE TO FINISH THE DARK, WITCHY APPEARANCE.

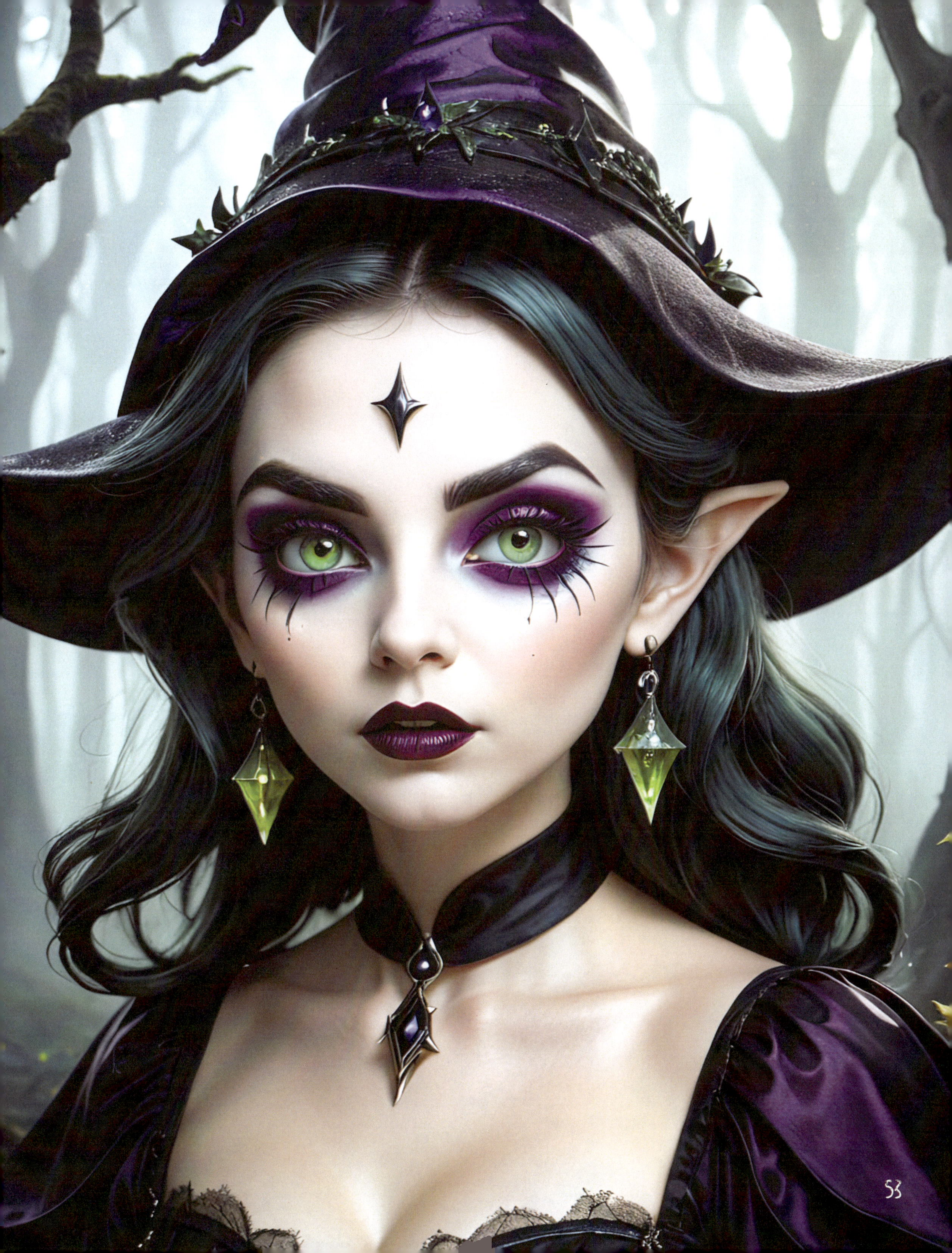

"MAD HATTER"

STEP-BY-STEP INSTRUCTIONS:

1. SKIN PREPARATION:

TOOLS: LIGHT FOUNDATION, CREAM BLUSH.

INSTRUCTIONS: APPLY LIGHT FOUNDATION ALL OVER THE FACE TO ACHIEVE A SMOOTH, PORCELAIN-LIKE COMPLEXION. APPLY CREAM BLUSH TO THE CHEEKS TO ADD A SOFT, ROSY FLUSH THAT ENHANCES THE ECCENTRIC APPEARANCE.

2. EYES:

TOOLS: PURPLE EYESHADOW, WHITE EYESHADOW, EYELINER, MASCARA, GREEN CONTACT LENSES.

INSTRUCTIONS: APPLY PURPLE EYESHADOW ON THE EYELIDS, BLENDING IT TOWARDS THE BROWS TO CREATE AN INTENSE, COLORFUL EFFECT. USE WHITE EYESHADOW ON THE INNER CORNERS OF THE EYES TO BRIGHTEN THEM AND ADD FRESHNESS TO THE GAZE. USE EYELINER TO DEFINE THE UPPER LASH LINE, THEN APPLY MASCARA TO LENGTHEN AND THICKEN THE LASHES. WEAR GREEN CONTACT LENSES TO GIVE THE EYES A MAD, WHIMSICAL LOOK.

3. EYEBROWS:

TOOLS: BROWN BROW POWDER OR PENCIL.

INSTRUCTIONS: DEFINE THE EYEBROWS, GIVING THEM A BOLD, SHARP SHAPE. THE BROWS SHOULD BE WELL-DEFINED TO CONTRAST WITH THE INTENSE EYE MAKEUP.

4. LIPS:

TOOLS: BRIGHT PINK LIPSTICK.

INSTRUCTIONS: APPLY BRIGHT PINK LIPSTICK, CAREFULLY OUTLINING THE LIPS. THE LIP COLOR SHOULD BE BOLD AND VIBRANT, MATCHING THE REST OF THE MAKEUP.

5. CHEEKS:

TOOLS: CREAM BLUSH.

INSTRUCTIONS: APPLY CREAM BLUSH TO THE CHEEKS TO ACHIEVE A PRONOUNCED FLUSH THAT EMPHASIZES THE ECCENTRIC CHARACTER.

6. FINISHING TOUCHES:

TOOLS: ORANGE WIG, MAD HATTER-STYLE HAT, ACCESSORIES (E.G., POLKA-DOT BOW TIE, COLORFUL EARRINGS).

INSTRUCTIONS: COMPLETE THE LOOK BY WEARING AN ORANGE WIG AND A MAD HATTER-STYLE HAT, GIVING THE CHARACTER A UNIQUE, WHIMSICAL APPEARANCE. ADD COLORFUL ACCESSORIES LIKE A POLKA-DOT BOW TIE AND EARRINGS TO FINISH THE MAD, FAIRY-TALE LOOK.

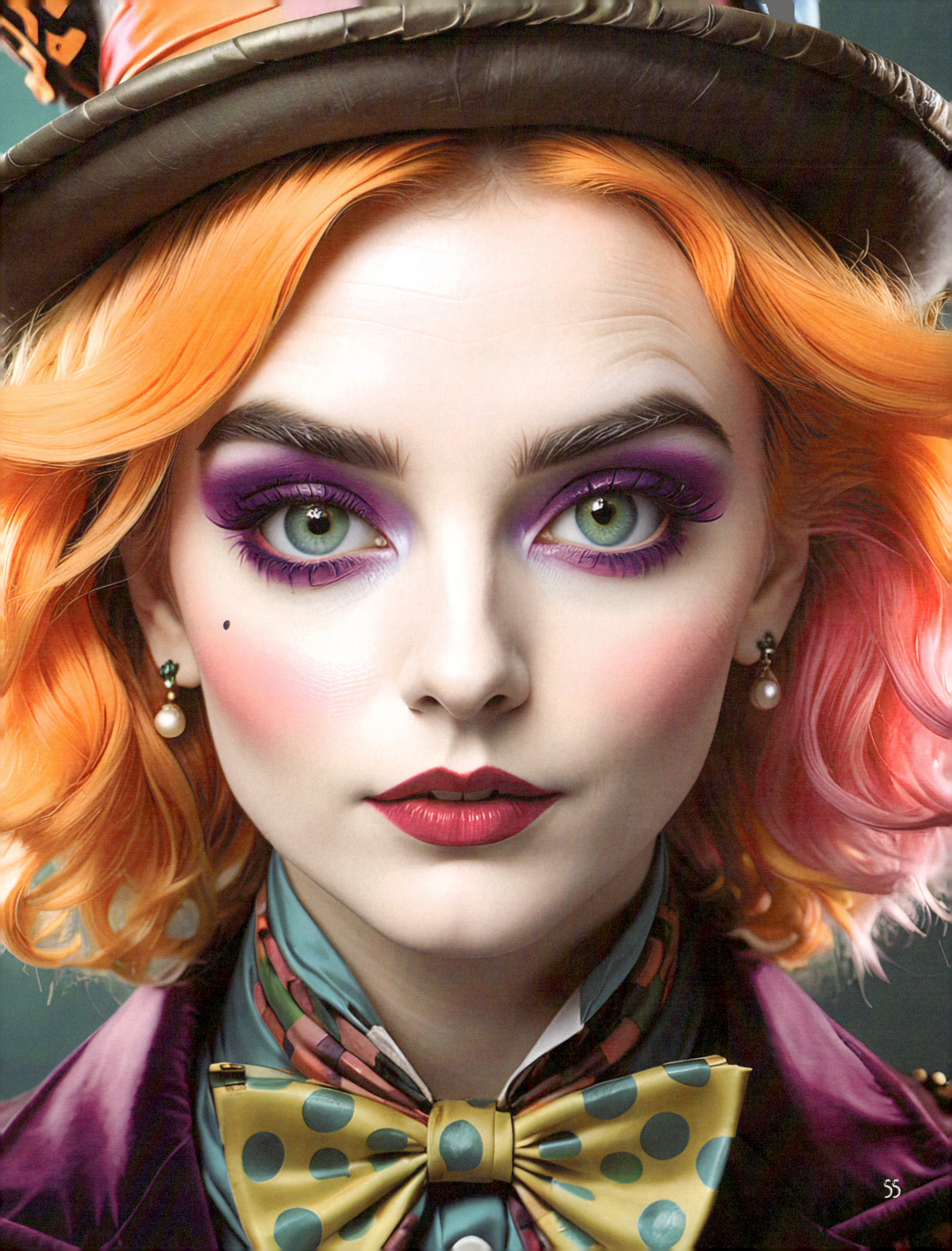

"BLOODY NURSE"

STEP-BY-STEP INSTRUCTIONS:

1. SKIN PREPARATION:

TOOLS: LIGHT FOUNDATION, TRANSLUCENT POWDER.

INSTRUCTIONS: APPLY LIGHT FOUNDATION ALL OVER THE FACE TO ACHIEVE A SMOOTH, PORCELAIN-LIKE COMPLEXION. ENSURE THE FOUNDATION IS EVENLY BLENDED, CREATING A PERFECT BASE FOR THE DRAMATIC MAKEUP.

2. EYES:

TOOLS: RED AND BLACK EYESHADOWS, BLACK EYELINER, MASCARA.

INSTRUCTIONS: APPLY RED EYESHADOW ON THE UPPER LID AND BLACK ON THE LOWER LID, BLENDING BOTH COLORS TO CREATE A DEEP, DRAMATIC EFFECT. USE BLACK EYELINER TO DEFINE THE UPPER AND LOWER LASH LINES. APPLY MASCARA TO ADD VOLUME AND LENGTH TO THE LASHES.

3. BLOODY TEARS:

TOOLS: RED FACE PAINT OR LIQUID RED EYELINER, FINE BRUSH.

INSTRUCTIONS: USE RED FACE PAINT OR LIQUID EYELINER TO CREATE DRIPPING, BLOODY TEARS COMING FROM UNDER THE EYES. THE LINES SHOULD BE IRREGULAR TO RESEMBLE NATURALLY FLOWING BLOOD.

4. EYEBROWS:

TOOLS: BLACK FACE PAINT OR EYELINER.

INSTRUCTIONS: DEFINE THE EYEBROWS, GIVING THEM A BOLD, SHARP SHAPE THAT CONTRASTS WITH THE INTENSE EYE MAKEUP.

5. LIPS:

TOOLS: RED LIPSTICK, LIP GLOSS.

INSTRUCTIONS: APPLY DEEP RED LIPSTICK, CAREFULLY OUTLINING THE LIPS. ADD GLOSS TO ENHANCE THE SHINE, AMPLIFYING THE DRAMATIC EFFECT OF THE MAKEUP.

6. FINISHING TOUCHES:

TOOLS: NURSE OUTFIT, SUCH AS A WHITE UNIFORM OR MEDICAL CAP.

INSTRUCTIONS: COMPLETE THE LOOK BY WEARING A CLASSIC NURSE OUTFIT, LIKE A WHITE UNIFORM OR A MEDICAL CAP. THE OUTFIT SHOULD BE SIMPLE TO CONTRAST WITH THE DRAMATIC MAKEUP.

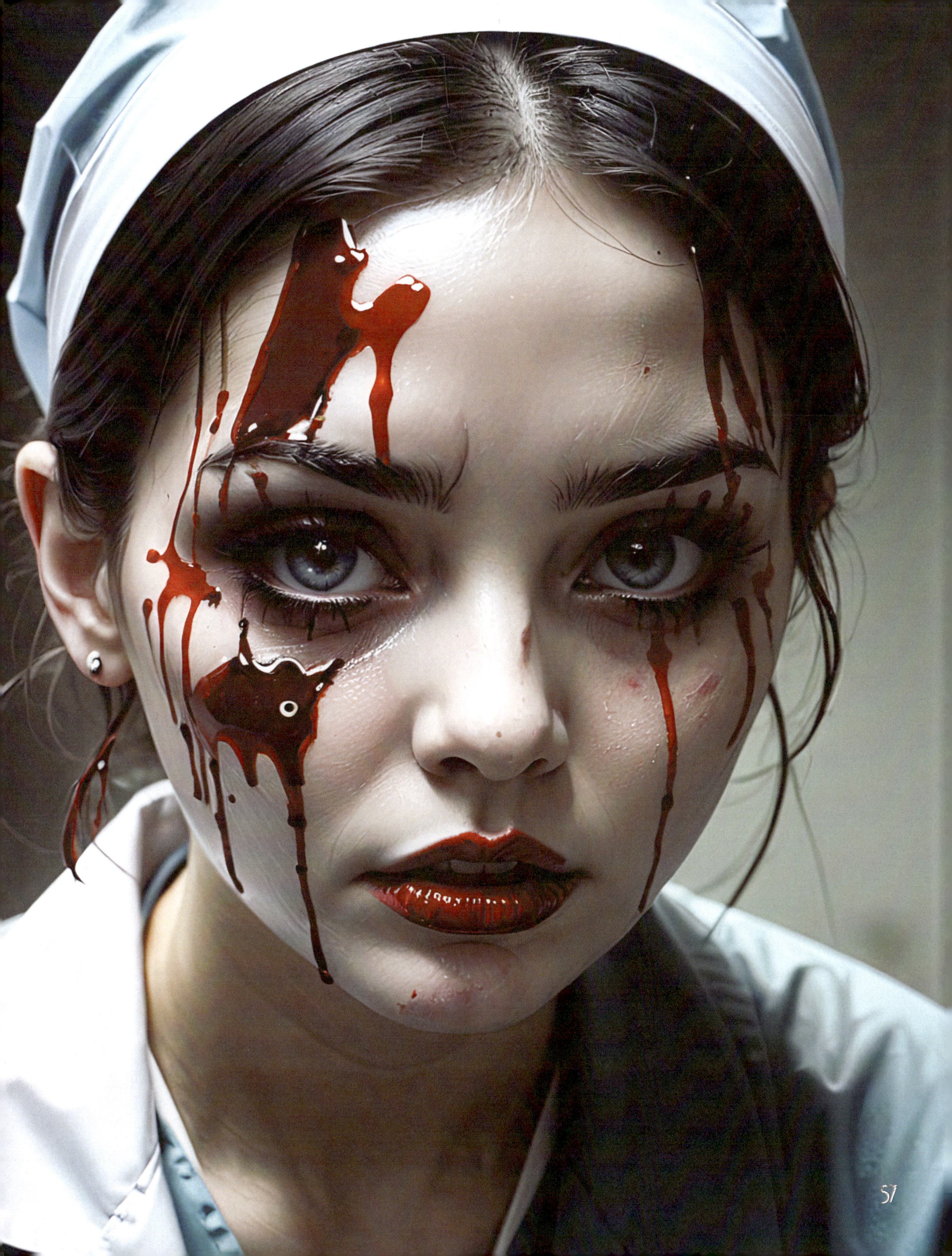

"ICE QUEEN"

STEP-BY-STEP INSTRUCTIONS:

1. SKIN PREPARATION:

TOOLS: LIGHT FOUNDATION, TRANSLUCENT POWDER.

INSTRUCTIONS: APPLY LIGHT FOUNDATION ALL OVER THE FACE TO ACHIEVE A SMOOTH, PORCELAIN-LIKE COMPLEXION. ENSURE THE FOUNDATION IS EVENLY BLENDED, THEN SET IT WITH TRANSLUCENT POWDER TO GIVE THE SKIN A MATTE, ICY FINISH.

2. EYES:

TOOLS: LIGHT BLUE EYESHADOW, WHITE EYESHADOW, MASCARA, BLUE CONTACT LENSES.

INSTRUCTIONS: APPLY LIGHT BLUE EYESHADOW ON THE UPPER LID, BLENDING IT TOWARDS THE BROWS TO CREATE A COOL, ICY EFFECT. USE WHITE EYESHADOW TO HIGHLIGHT THE INNER CORNERS OF THE EYES. APPLY MASCARA TO ADD LENGTH AND VOLUME TO THE LASHES. FINALLY, WEAR BLUE CONTACT LENSES TO GIVE THE EYES AN ICY, MESMERIZING LOOK.

3. EYEBROWS:

TOOLS: LIGHT GRAY BROW POWDER OR PENCIL.

INSTRUCTIONS: DEFINE THE EYEBROWS, GIVING THEM A SUBTLE YET PRONOUNCED SHAPE. THE BROWS SHOULD BE GENTLY DEFINED TO COMPLEMENT THE ICY EYE MAKEUP.

4. LIPS:

TOOLS: LIGHT PINK LIPSTICK.

INSTRUCTIONS: APPLY LIGHT PINK LIPSTICK, CAREFULLY OUTLINING THE LIPS. THE LIPS SHOULD APPEAR SOFT AND NATURAL, ENHANCING THE ICY, ROYAL APPEARANCE.

5. DETAILS:

TOOLS: SILVER GLITTER, COSMETIC ADHESIVE.

INSTRUCTIONS: USE SILVER GLITTER TO ADD SUBTLE, SHIMMERING ACCENTS AROUND THE EYES AND ON THE CHEEKS. YOU CAN ALSO ADD GLITTER ALONG THE HAIRLINE AND ON THE DéCOLLETAGE TO ENHANCE THE FROSTY QUEEN EFFECT.

6. FINISHING TOUCHES:

TOOLS: WHITE WIG OR SILVER HAIR STYLING, ACCESSORIES (E.G., SNOWFLAKE-THEMED EARRINGS AND NECKLACE).

INSTRUCTIONS: COMPLETE THE LOOK BY WEARING A WHITE WIG OR STYLING THE HAIR IN SILVER. ADD ACCESSORIES LIKE SNOWFLAKE-THEMED EARRINGS AND A NECKLACE TO COMPLETE THE ICE QUEEN APPEARANCE.

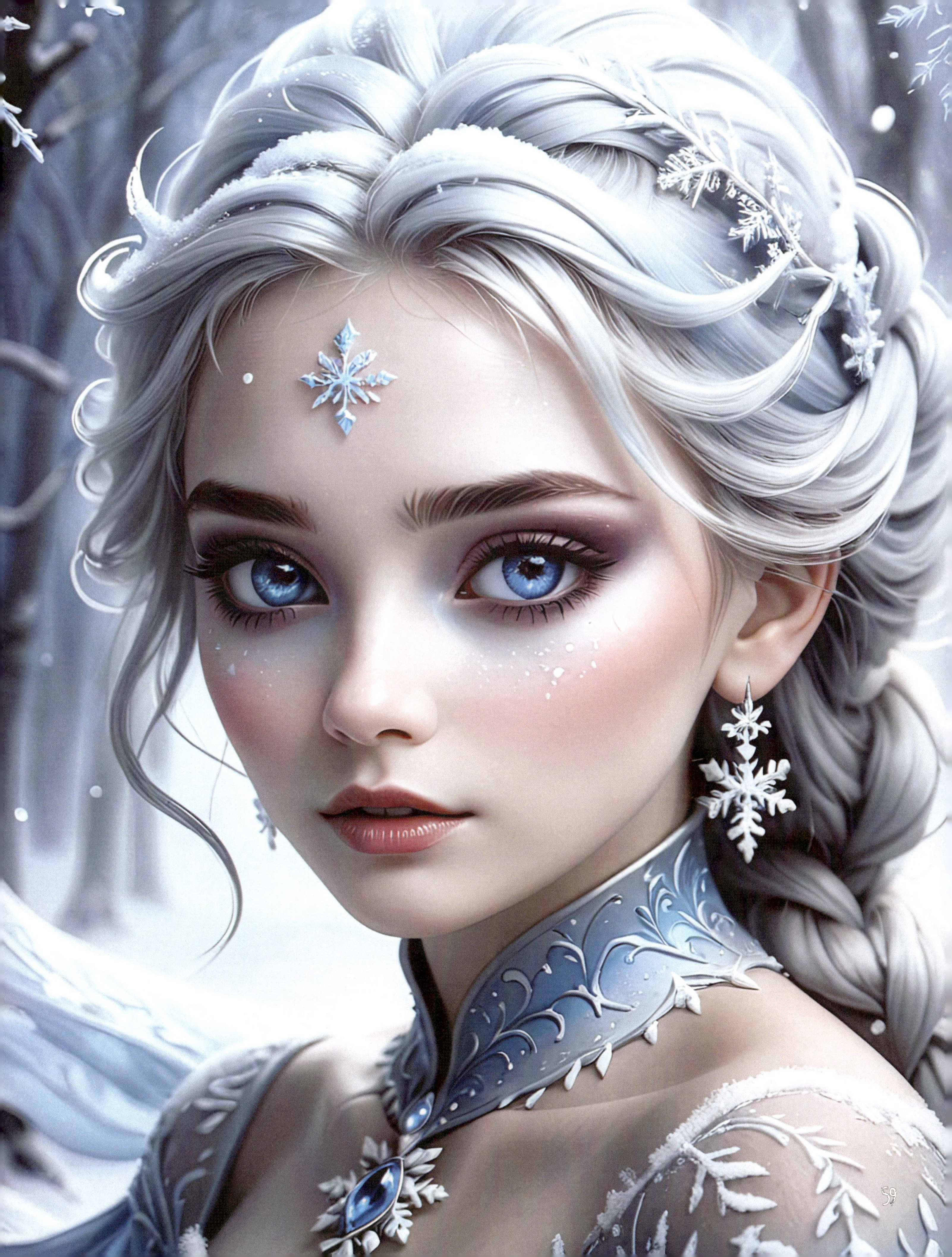

"DRAGON WARRIOR"

STEP-BY-STEP INSTRUCTIONS:

1. SKIN PREPARATION:

TOOLS: LIGHT FOUNDATION, TRANSLUCENT POWDER.

INSTRUCTIONS: APPLY LIGHT FOUNDATION ALL OVER THE FACE TO ACHIEVE A SMOOTH, EVEN COMPLEXION. ENSURE THE FOUNDATION IS EVENLY BLENDED, CREATING A PERFECT BASE FOR THE DRAGON SCALE MAKEUP.

2. DRAGON SCALES ON THE FACE:

TOOLS: GREEN AND GOLD FACE PAINT, DETAIL BRUSH, SCALE STENCIL (OPTIONAL).

INSTRUCTIONS: APPLY GREEN FACE PAINT TO THE CENTRAL PART OF THE FACE, PARTICULARLY ON THE FOREHEAD, CHEEKS, AND CHIN, CREATING A DRAGON SCALE PATTERN. IF YOU WANT A MORE DETAILED EFFECT, YOU CAN USE A SCALE STENCIL TO APPLY THE PATTERN. THEN, ADD ACCENTS OF GOLD PAINT TO HIGHLIGHT THE EDGES OF THE SCALES AND GIVE THEM A SHIMMERING EFFECT.

3. EYES:

TOOLS: GREEN EYESHADOW, BLACK EYELINER, MASCARA, GREEN CONTACT LENSES.

INSTRUCTIONS: APPLY GREEN EYESHADOW ON THE EYELIDS, BLENDING IT TOWARDS THE TEMPLES TO CREATE AN INTENSE, DRAGON-LIKE EFFECT. USE BLACK EYELINER TO DRAW A BOLD LINE ON THE UPPER LID. APPLY MASCARA TO ENHANCE THE LASHES, THEN WEAR GREEN CONTACT LENSES TO GIVE THE GAZE A HYPNOTIC, DRAGON-LIKE APPEARANCE.

4. EYEBROWS:

TOOLS: DARK GREEN BROW POWDER OR PENCIL.

INSTRUCTIONS: DEFINE THE EYEBROWS, GIVING THEM A BOLD, SHARP SHAPE. THE BROWS SHOULD BE WELL-DEFINED TO COMPLEMENT THE INTENSE EYE MAKEUP.

5. LIPS:

TOOLS: LIGHT PINK LIPSTICK OR LIP BALM.

INSTRUCTIONS: APPLY LIGHT PINK LIPSTICK OR BALM TO THE LIPS TO GIVE THEM A SUBTLE COLOR THAT WON'T DISTRACT FROM THE DRAGON SCALES AND EYES.

6. FINISHING TOUCHES:

TOOLS: GREEN WIG OR HAIR STYLED GREEN, FAKE HORNS OR DRAGON ACCESSORIES, ARMOR.

INSTRUCTIONS: COMPLETE THE LOOK BY WEARING A GREEN WIG OR STYLING THE HAIR IN GREEN. YOU CAN ADD FAKE HORNS TO ENHANCE THE DRAGON LOOK AND WEAR ARMOR OR DRAGON ACCESSORIES TO COMPLETE THE WARRIOR CHARACTER.

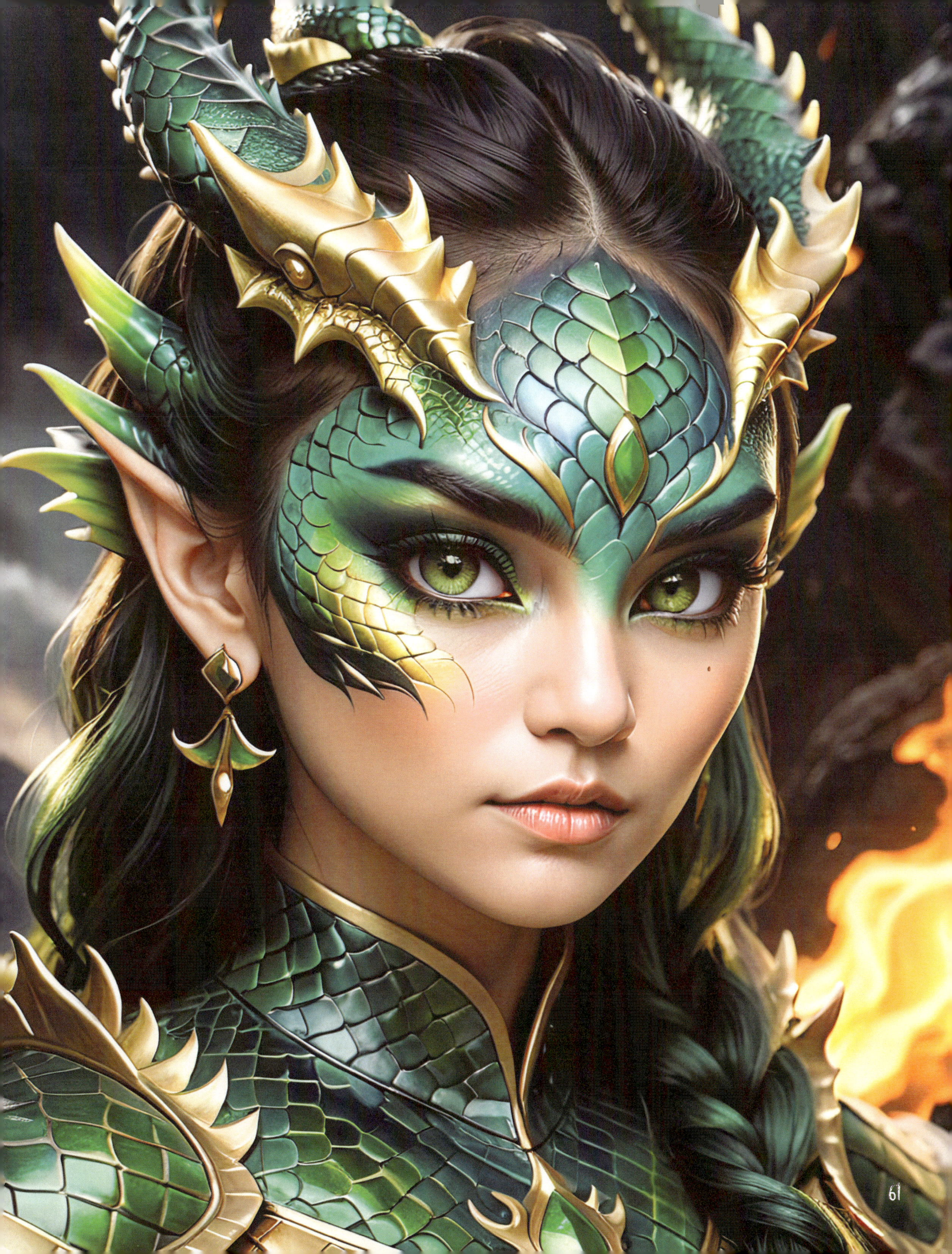

"DIABOLIC JESTER"

STEP-BY-STEP INSTRUCTIONS:

1. SKIN PREPARATION:

TOOLS: WHITE FACE PAINT, SPONGE OR BRUSH FOR APPLICATION, TRANSLUCENT POWDER.

INSTRUCTIONS: APPLY WHITE FACE PAINT ALL OVER THE FACE TO ACHIEVE A SMOOTH, UNIFORM BASE. ENSURE THE PAINT IS EVENLY BLENDED, CREATING A CLEAN, CONSISTENT LAYER. SET THE MAKEUP WITH TRANSLUCENT POWDER TO PREVENT SMUDGING.

2. EYES:

TOOLS: BLACK EYESHADOW, RED EYESHADOW, BLACK EYELINER, MASCARA, RED CONTACT LENSES.

INSTRUCTIONS: APPLY BLACK EYESHADOW ON THE EYELIDS, BLENDING IT TOWARDS THE TEMPLES TO CREATE AN INTENSE, DARK EFFECT. ADD RED EYESHADOW ON THE LOWER LID, BLENDING THE COLORS FOR CONTRAST. USE BLACK EYELINER TO DRAW BOLD LINES AROUND THE EYES. APPLY MASCARA TO ENHANCE THE LASHES, THEN WEAR RED CONTACT LENSES TO GIVE THE EYES A DIABOLIC LOOK.

3. DIABOLIC PATTERNS ON THE FACE:

TOOLS: BLACK AND RED FACE PAINT, FINE BRUSH.

INSTRUCTIONS: USE BLACK AND RED FACE PAINT TO DRAW DISTINCTIVE PATTERNS ON THE FACE, SUCH AS DIAMONDS, SPIKES, AND LINES, EMPHASIZING THE JESTER'S DIABOLIC APPEARANCE. THE PATTERNS SHOULD BE SYMMETRICAL AND PRONOUNCED.

4. EYEBROWS:

TOOLS: BLACK FACE PAINT OR EYELINER.

INSTRUCTIONS: DEFINE THE EYEBROWS, GIVING THEM A BOLD, CURVED SHAPE THAT ADDS A SINISTER EXPRESSION TO THE FACE. THE EYEBROWS SHOULD BE WELL-DEFINED TO ACCENTUATE THE INTENSE EYE MAKEUP.

5. LIPS:

TOOLS: RED LIPSTICK.

INSTRUCTIONS: APPLY BRIGHT RED LIPSTICK, OUTLINING THE LIPS INTO A CHARACTERISTIC, WIDE JESTER'S SMILE. YOU CAN ALSO ADD SOME SHADED LINES ON THE SIDES OF THE MOUTH TO EMPHASIZE THE EFFECT OF A DEMONIC GRIN.

6. FINISHING TOUCHES:

TOOLS: BLACK-RED WIG OR HAIR STYLING, DIABOLIC HORNS OR OTHER ACCESSORIES, JESTER COSTUME.

INSTRUCTIONS: COMPLETE THE LOOK BY WEARING A BLACK-RED WIG OR STYLING THE HAIR ACCORDINGLY. ADD DIABOLIC HORNS TO ENHANCE THE EFFECT, AND WEAR A CLASSIC JESTER COSTUME IN SHADES OF BLACK AND RED. ACCESSORIES LIKE A NECKLACE OR EARRINGS WITH A RED DIAMOND MOTIF WILL COMPLETE THE SINISTER APPEARANCE.

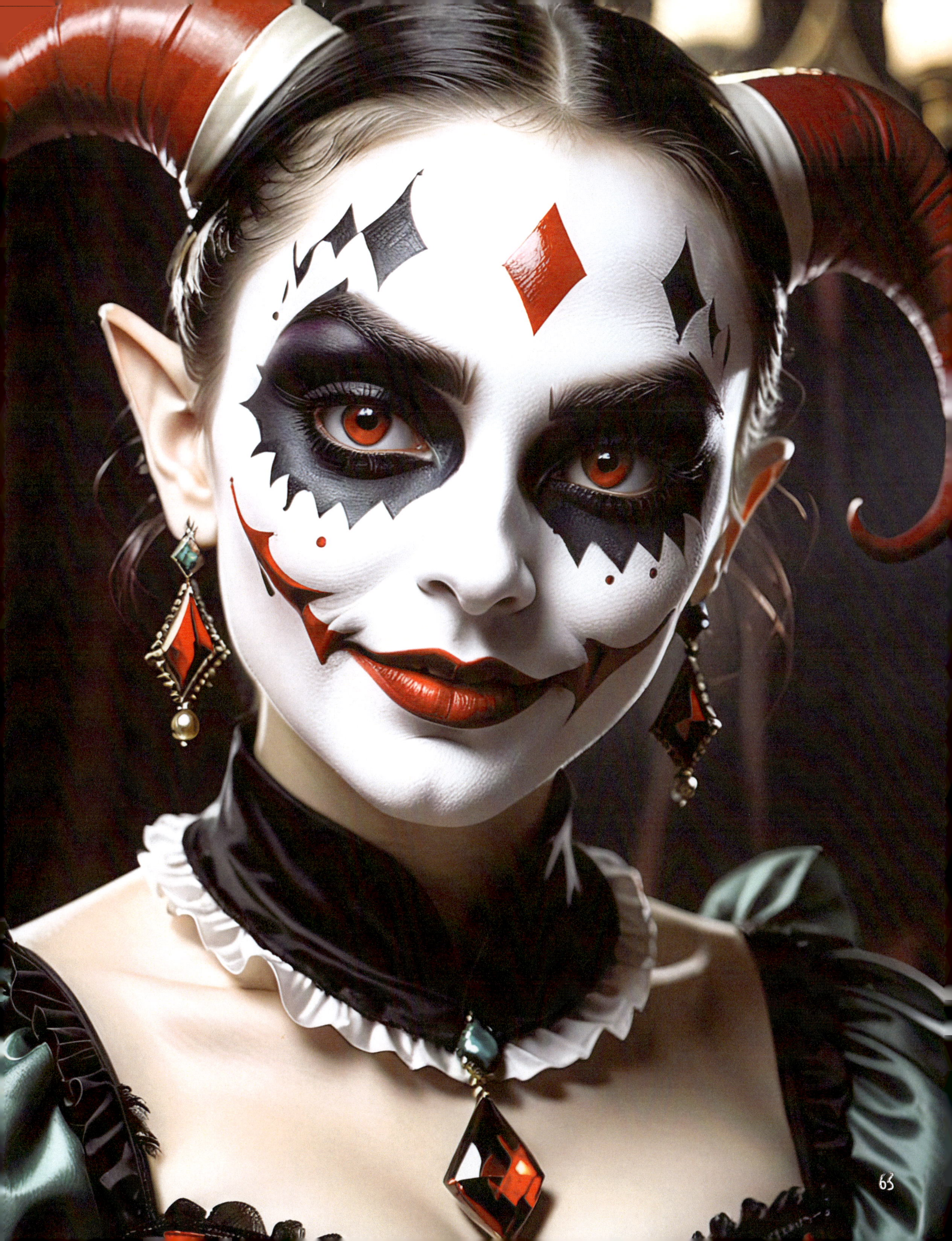

"DEVIL QUEEN"

STEP-BY-STEP INSTRUCTIONS:

1. SKIN PREPARATION:

TOOLS: LIGHT FOUNDATION, TRANSLUCENT POWDER.

INSTRUCTIONS: APPLY LIGHT FOUNDATION ALL OVER THE FACE TO ACHIEVE A SMOOTH, EVEN COMPLEXION. ENSURE THE FOUNDATION IS EVENLY BLENDED, CREATING A PERFECT BASE FOR THE DRAMATIC, DEVILISH MAKEUP.

2. EYES:

TOOLS: RED EYESHADOW, BLACK EYELINER, MASCARA, ORANGE CONTACT LENSES.

INSTRUCTIONS: APPLY RED EYESHADOW ON THE EYELIDS, BLENDING IT OUTWARD TO CREATE AN INTENSE, FIERY EFFECT. USE BLACK EYELINER TO DRAW A BOLD LINE ON THE UPPER LID, EXTENDING IT TOWARDS THE OUTER CORNERS OF THE EYES. APPLY MASCARA TO ENHANCE THE LASHES, THEN WEAR ORANGE CONTACT LENSES TO GIVE THE GAZE A FLAMING, DEMONIC APPEARANCE.

3. DEVILISH PATTERNS ON THE FACE:

TOOLS: RED AND BLACK FACE PAINT, FINE BRUSH.

INSTRUCTIONS: USE RED FACE PAINT TO CREATE DRAMATIC PATTERNS AROUND THE EYES AND ON THE FOREHEAD, RESEMBLING FLAMES OR BAT WINGS. USE BLACK PAINT TO ADD DETAILS THAT EMPHASIZE THE SHAPE OF THE PATTERNS AND GIVE THEM DEPTH.

4. EYEBROWS:

TOOLS: BLACK FACE PAINT OR EYELINER.

INSTRUCTIONS: DEFINE THE EYEBROWS, GIVING THEM A SHARP, DRAMATIC SHAPE THAT COMPLEMENTS THE DEVILISH PATTERNS AROUND THE EYES. THE EYEBROWS SHOULD BE WELL-DEFINED TO ACCENTUATE THE INTENSE CHARACTER OF THE MAKEUP.

5. LIPS:

TOOLS: RED LIPSTICK.

INSTRUCTIONS: APPLY BRIGHT RED LIPSTICK, CAREFULLY OUTLINING THE LIPS. THE LIPS SHOULD LOOK BOLD AND DRAMATIC, MATCHING THE REST OF THE MAKEUP.

6. FINISHING TOUCHES:

TOOLS: BLACK WIG OR HAIR STYLED BLACK, FAKE HORNS, ACCESSORIES (E.G., FLAME-SHAPED EARRINGS AND NECKLACE).

INSTRUCTIONS: COMPLETE THE LOOK BY WEARING A BLACK WIG OR STYLING THE HAIR IN BLACK. ADD FAKE HORNS TO ENHANCE THE DEVILISH LOOK, AND WEAR ACCESSORIES LIKE FLAME-SHAPED EARRINGS AND A NECKLACE TO COMPLETE THE FIERY, DEMONIC APPEARANCE.

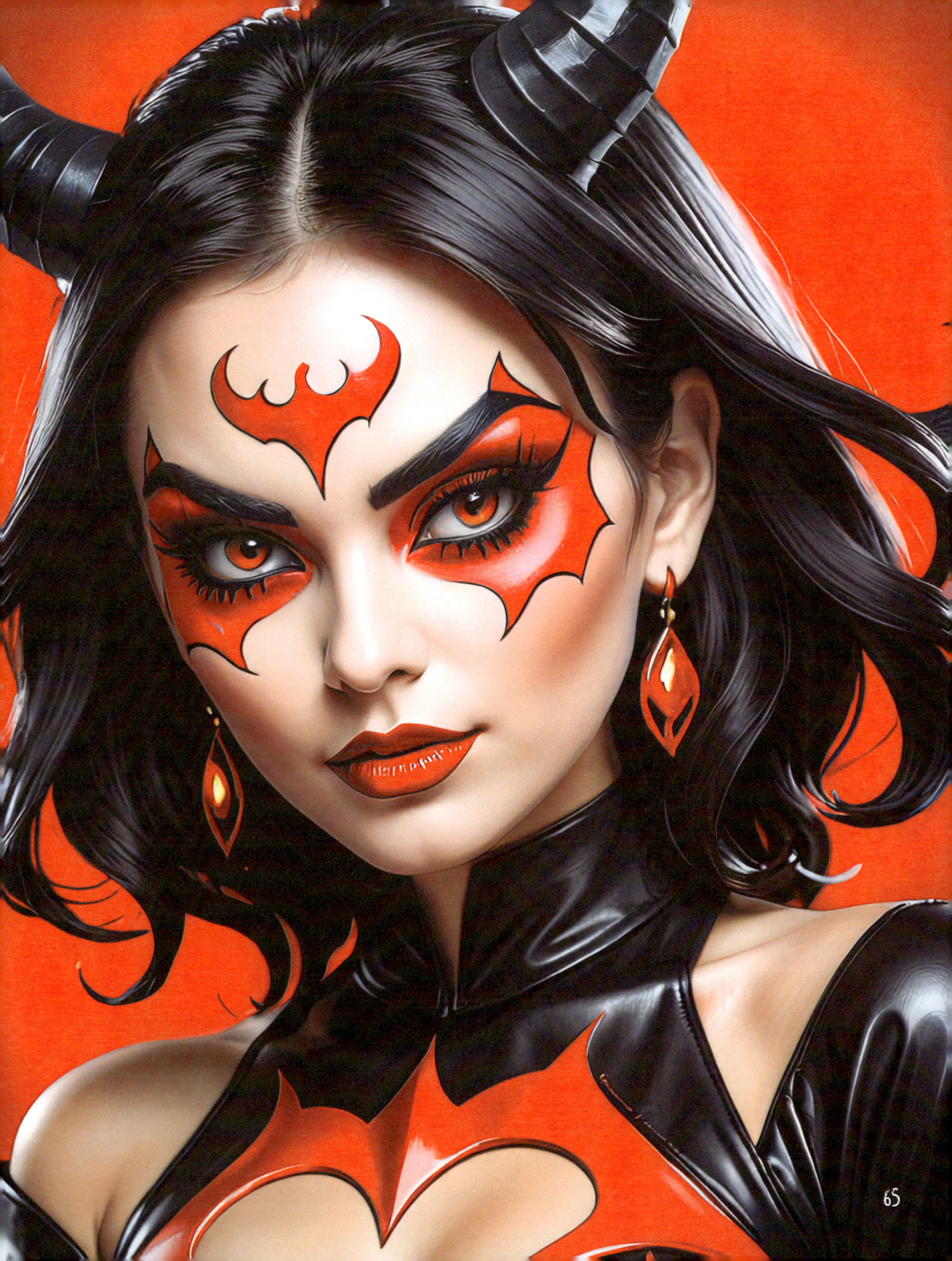

THANK YOU FOR CHOOSING OUR BOOK AND FOR DIVING INTO THE WORLD OF HALLOWEEN MAKEUP.

WE HOPE THAT OUR INSTRUCTIONS, INSPIRATIONS, AND TIPS HAVE HELPED YOU CREATE UNFORGETTABLE LOOKS THAT ADDED MAGIC AND THRILLS TO YOUR HALLOWEEN CELEBRATIONS. EACH PROJECT IN THIS BOOK WAS CRAFTED WITH YOU IN MIND — YOUR CREATIVITY, YOUR PASSION, AND YOUR DESIRE TO EXPLORE NEW AND EXCITING WAYS TO EXPRESS YOURSELF.

REMEMBER, MAKEUP IS AN ART FORM WITHOUT LIMITS. EVERY BRUSHSTROKE, EVERY DETAIL IS AN OPPORTUNITY TO CREATE SOMETHING UNIQUE THAT REFLECTS YOUR PERSONALITY AND IMAGINATION. LET THIS BOOK BE AN INSPIRATION FOR YOU FOR YEARS TO COME, ENCOURAGING FURTHER EXPERIMENTATION AND DISCOVERY OF NEW TECHNIQUES.

ONCE AGAIN, THANK YOU FOR PURCHASING OUR BOOK. YOUR SUPPORT ALLOWS US TO CONTINUE CREATING MATERIALS THAT HELP YOU GROW AND ENJOY THE ART OF MAKEUP. WE WISH YOU MANY JOYFUL AND CREATIVE MOMENTS WITH MAKEUP, AND MANY SCARY AND UNFORGETTABLE HALLOWEENS!